SOMETHING WILD
COOKBOOK

WRITTEN BY
RICHARD M. GAUERKE

Layout Design and Typesetting
Tim Christensen

Illustrations
Michael T. Burch
&
Jeff Essler

c/o

Ca

D1206559

The Printery
Plains, Montana

Dedicated to Dad
He encouraged me to make it happen.

CONTENTS

INTRODUCTION

The early inhabitants of this country lived entirely off the land. They harvested game, fruit, berries in its natural state. When nature was bountiful, they thrived, when not, they persevered or moved on.

Today, with the focus on cultivation, conservation and the attempts to maintain the delicate balance of nature, we have the opportunity to enjoy wild bounty of unequaled quantity and quality. Deer herds have flourished. Anglers annually catch increasing numbers of fish. The import of game birds and successful management of waterfowl offers superb challenges afield.

However, today's sportsman is in pursuit of the experience, not the sustenance. "Return the resource" has replaced the mindset of "fill the freezer." Future generations depend on our ability to preserve and conserve. Therefore, it is with this mission that today's sportsman accept the legacy of our ancestors. The self-sufficient feeling that accompanies the wild harvest is our inheritance. The bounty that makes the feast is ours to protect and enjoy.

Cooking techniques have changed over the years. We've graduated from the sticks and fire method and today's kitchen can be equipped with appliances to roast, steam, grill, poach and fry. While one of my favorite memories includes stick roasting elk tenderloin over an open fire on a high mountain, I prefer the convenience of my kitchen to achieve the goodness a once wild inhabitant deserves.

In this book I have attempted to offer a variety of methods for preparing fish, big game and fowl as well as berries and other wild plants. It was my objective to present recipes which are simple, practical, and yet tasty. In some instances I've become somewhat elaborate, maybe even carried away a bit, but I've always tried to create a feast to compliment the nobility of nature.

Generally I prefer not to use exotic herbs and spices and unlike many creators of recipes for wild game, I never use larding as a means of enhancing moisture or masking the natural flavor of meat or fish. Furthermore, with today's emphasis on diet, cholesterol and restricted fat intake, I work to enhance flavor through means other than increased fat. To assist you in your selection, recipes with reduced fat and calorie content will be marked "on the lighter side" throughout this book.

I trust that you will enjoy this book and its contents. Special thanks go out to my many friends who contributed recipes, game, and appetites so your experience of **Something Wild** will be truly enjoyable.

FISH

North America is one gigantic, prolific fishery. I believe more time is spent in search of fish than any other recreational pursuit, and, with good reason. Fishing offers something for everyone. North country walleye, pacific salmon, southern catfish, bass, western trout, and panfish everywhere offer anglers young and old excitement, adventure, and superb eating. Furthermore, fish and fishing is good for you. The tranquil effects of a quiet lake coupled with the taste and aroma of fresh cooked fish soothes the spirit and puts life in perspective.

For many years I thought "fried" was the only way to prepare fish. Growing up in Wisconsin with the traditional "Friday fish fry" strengthened that belief. However, over the years I've enjoyed using different methods to prepare a variety of fresh and saltwater fish and now view frying as one option to quality dining.

The size of your catch is a major factor in preparing fish. Although catch and release of the big spawners is gaining popularity among sporting enthusiasts, occasionally a big one finds its way into your creel. Big fish are rarely fried. Your alternatives are baking, boiling, poaching, broiling, and of course canning and pickling. Chowders and fish soups and stews are also fun to try. This leads one to realize the versatility of fish.

Fish as with any wild inhabitant should be properly cared for from the moment they are caught. That means putting on ice until they can be properly cleaned. Fish not eaten soon after catching should be frozen. Fish will sustain their quality in the freezer for longer periods of time if you package them in milk cartons filled with water, and the tops stapled shut. After the water freezes, these containers can be stacked to economize freezer space.

ORIGINAL FISH BATTER

Whether you're breaking for a shore lunch or entertaining friends at home, this tasty way to prepare fresh fish will have your friends returning for more.

1/2 cup corn meal
1/2 cup corn starch
1/4 cup flour
2 egg whites
2 teaspoon baking powder
1/2 teaspoon salt
1/4 teaspoon pepper
1 cup beer

Mix dry ingredients with beer, in separate bowl beat egg whites until stiff, fold into batter.

Pat fillets dry, then dip in batter. Fry in deep fat or peanut oil heats to 370˚ for 5 to 8 minutes or until fish turns a golden brown.

Drain on absorbent paper and serve hot.

WINNEBAGO GRILLED WALLEYE

A tasty meal that is easy to prepare and very popular when fried isn't.

walleye fillets with bones removed, skin and scales left on.
butter
salt

Grill fillets covered, skin side down on well greased rack, 3-4 inches above the coals for 5-8 minutes. Baste with butter, salt and pepper to taste.

DEVILS LAKE PAN FRIED PERCH FILLETS

If there truly is a perch heaven it must be Devils Lake in North Dakota where the perch are fat, tasty and plentiful.

1 package finely crushed saltine crackers
2 eggs
2/3 cup beer
1/2 teaspoon salt
1/4 teaspoon pepper

Beat eggs, add beer, salt and pepper and mix thoroughly.

Dip fillets in egg beer mixture, roll in crushed crackers then place in frying pan. Turn only once, as soon as the first side is golden brown. Generally required cooking time will be from 3 to 5 minutes per side. Total cooking time will depend on the thickness of the fillet.

MISSOURI RIVER LING CHOWDER

While the ling isn't the prettiest fish in the waters, this fresh water cousin to the cod can, with the right preparation, grace your table and make believers of friends and family.

1/8 lb. butter
1/2 lb. bacon strips cut into 1 1/2 pieces
2 large onions sliced
2 large potatoes peeled and sliced into 1/2 inch pieces
1 quart fish stock
1 pint cream
1 1/2-2 lbs. ling cut into 1 inch chunks
paprika
pepper

Use only the flesh above the lateral line, this can easily be skinned and cut away from the backbone.

In a large (6-8 quarts) pot melt butter over medium heat. Add bacon and onion and sauté until soft. Add potatoes and mix to coat with butter. Pour fish stock and simmer about 15 minutes or until potatoes are almost cooked. Reduce heat, and add cream. Heat until steaming (never boil) stirring frequently. Add fish and cook until done approx. 5 minutes. Sprinkle with paprika and pepper.

Serve with fresh baked bread.

STUFFED BAKED WALLEYE

Try this elegant, mouthwatering recipe when a special, festive treat is called for.

1- 6 to 8 lb. walleye scaled, cleaned and gills removed
1 tablespoon lemon juice
8 slices fresh bread
1 medium onion
2 stalks celery
6 oz. fresh mushrooms sliced
1- 6 oz. canned crab meat
1/4 cup butter or margarine
1 teaspoon salt
1/8 teaspoon black pepper

Preheat oven to 425°. Rub inside of fish with salt and sprinkle with lemon juice. Cut bread into 1/4 inch cubes. Finely dice onion and celery. Combine all ingredients and mix well. Fill fish cavity with stuffing and fasten with skewers and string. Wrap in foil and bake in a shallow pan for 40 minutes. Open foil and bake 15 minutes longer, baste with butter during the last 15 minutes.

GRILLED WALLEYE WITH VEGETABLES

For a quick change of pace this recipe can be equally welcome at the campsite or dinner table.

4 medium walleye fillets
2 tablespoons melted butter
salt/pepper

vegetable mixture:
2 cups shredded carrots
2 cups chopped broccoli
1/2 cup finely diced onion
1/3 cup grated parmesan cheese
1/4 cup water
2 tablespoons melted butter or margarine

For each fillet use a sheet of heavy duty aluminum foil approx. 14X14 inches. Brush both sides of fillet with butter and place in the center of the foil, sprinkle with salt and pepper. Combine the vegetable mixture. Place approx. 1/2 cup of the vegetable mixture on each side of the fillet (1 cup total per fillet) bring the two sides of foil together over the fish, fold leaving ample room for steam circulation. Fold and crimp ends. Cook in covered grill over medium hot coals for approx. 15 minutes or until the fish flakes easily at the thickest part.

Oven method: bake at 350 for 25 to 30 minutes. Remove from oven and let sit for several minutes, open carefully and let steam escape before serving.

SALMON SUPREME

(2 Servings)

One bite of this sportsmans rendition of eggs bendict will take you back to your favorite stream where once again you'll battle the mighty salmon.

2 english muffins split
2 tablespoons butter
4 eggs
1/4 teaspoon salt
1/4 teaspoon paprika
1 green onion (use green part only) thinly sliced
1/2 cup skinned and boned smoked salmon broken into small chunks
dash of pepper

Using a small bowl, beat eggs with salt and pepper, melt butter in frying pan or double boiler. Add eggs and cook slowly, stirring frequently until done with a creamy consistency.

Simultaneously toast english muffins, butter lightly and divide salmon on each muffin. Spoon the eggs over the salmon, sprinkle with paprika and top with finely chopped onions.

WINNECONNE ORANGE BUTTERED BASS

*When the Spring run is on, this respite from traditional frying
will get the attention of your guests.*

**2 lbs. of whitebass fillet
2 tablespoons grated orange zest (the colorful outer coating of the
fruit)
2 teaspoons grated lemon zest
2 tablespoons minced green onion
1 1/2 tablespoons minced parsley
6 tablespoons butter
salt and pepper**

Preheat the oven to 350°. Butter a shallow baking dish large enough to hold the fish in a single layer. Season the fish on both sides with salt and pepper; arrange in the baking dish, sprinkle the Lemon and Orange zest, onion and minced parsley evenly over the fish.

Bake for 15 to 18 minutes, basting several times until fish flakes easily at its thickest part.

GREAT LAKES FISH BOIL

The fish boil lends versatility to preparing your catch. The salmon isn't the only fish you can use, any large fish will boil nicely.

per person:
1 lb. steaked salmon
1 medium onion, quartered
1 medium potato scrubbed (with peel) quartered
1 stalk celery
1 carrot
1 teaspoon caraway seed (optional)
salt
drawn butter
Lemon

When serving a crowd, a trout or salmon kettle is a necessity but your soup kettle or canner will easily accommodate the fixins for up to 6 adults.

Heat the potatoes, carrots, onions and celery in 6-8 quarts of water (depending on the size of your container) bring to a boil and boil for 15 minutes. Place the fish steaks in a basket or cheesecloth bag and lower into the boiling water above the vegetables. Add 1/2 cup salt. Cover and boil for 12 minutes.

The flakes should easily separate when tested with a fork. Remove the fish, drain off the vegetable water. Serve vegetables and fish with drawn butter and lemon.

GRILLED SALMON FILLETS

1 6-8 lb. salmon filleted and boned leaving skin on
1/2 cup butter melted
1/8 teaspoon garlic powder
salt and pepper

Grill fillets covered, skin side down on a well greased rack, 3-4 inches above the coals for 15-18 minutes. Combine melted butter and garlic powder and baste twice during the cooking process. Fish will be done when it flakes easily at its thickest part. Salt to taste.

For a change in taste, baste with your favorite barbeque sauce about 2 minutes before removing from grill.

NORTHERN FILLETS IN CREAM

4 thick fillets (about 1/2 lb. each)
4 tablespoons butter
2 medium onions, diced
1/4 teaspoon salt
1 cup white wine
2 cups cream
2 tablespoons cornstarch
paprika

Melt the butter in a heavy skillet and lightly sauté the onions until soft. Sprinkle salt on both sides of the fillets and place in pan on top of the onions. Pour wine over fish and simmer for 3 to 4 minutes, add cream, thicken with cornstarch, cover the pan and cook over low heat 12-14 minutes or until it flakes easily at its thickest part. Just before serving sprinkle with paprika.

PACIFIC BAKED SALMON

1 8-10 lb. Salmon cleaned and gills removed
1 medium onion, sliced
1/2 stick butter
1 lemon, sliced
1 teaspoon salt

Preheat oven to 350°. Rub inside of fish with salt and butter and arrange lemon and onion slices. Rub outside of fish with butter, wrap in heavy duty aluminum foil and bake for 1 hour.

For a truly exquisite delight serve with a Norwegian butter sauce made from:

1 stick butter
1 teaspoon finely minced garlic
1 medium onion, finely minced
1/3 cup white wine
1/2 teaspoon paprika
1/2 teaspoon koerner style hot mustard
1/2 teaspoon lemon juice
1 bay leaf
1/2 teaspoon corn starch
1 cup fish stock

Using a medium sauce pan, melt butter and lightly sauté onion and garlic until soft. Stir in wine, paprika, mustard, bay leaf, and lemon juice. Mix corn starch in fish stock, add to sauce pan. Salt and pepper to taste. Slowly cook over medium heat until sauce thickens.

TANGY FISH SALAD

Use fish which are light and flakey, such as bass, walleye, or snapper.

with each cup of flaked fish, mix 1/2 cup finely chopped or grated raw carrot
1 1/2 cup diced spinach
1 green onion, finely minced
1/2 stalk celery, diced
1/4 cup bean sprouts

for the dressing blend:
1/4 cup mayonnaise
1 tablespoon tarragon vinegar
1 teaspoon lemon juice

Combine all ingredients, mix with dressing. Shape desired portions on a bed of fresh lettuce and sprinkle with paprika.

POOR MAN'S LOBSTER

2 lbs. torsk, cod, muskie fillets
1 teaspoon salt
1 bayleaf
1 onion
2 lemon slices
1/2 cup white wine

Place fish in kettle with enough water to cover, add salt, bayleaf, onion, lemon and wine. Bring to boil, reduce heat, simmer for 12 minutes. Carefully remove fish

Serve with drawn butter, sprinkle with chopped parsley.

NORTHWEST BROILED SALMON CHUNKS

1 7-10 lb. salmon, cleaned, filleted
1 tablespoon crushed peppercorns
1 bay leaf
1 tablespoon dried celery leaves
2 tablespoons salt
1 medium onion finely diced
1/2 cup sour cream
parmesan cheese

Combine peppercorns, bay leaf, celery and salt in large kettle of boiling water. Cut salmon in 1 1/2 inch chunks and add to the boiling mixture. Lower heat and simmer gently for 6 to 7 minutes or until nearly done. Remove fish from water, place in shallow baking dish. Sprinkle with lemon juice, onion, and spread with sour cream. Sprinkle with parmesan cheese. Place low in broiler and broil slowly until hot and turning a tinged brown.

BUTTERED STUFFED SNAPPER

Snapper are not only fun to catch, but fun to work with in the kitchen. This recipe will allow you to show off your skills.

5 tablespoons butter
1 teaspoon basil leaves
3/4 teaspoon onion powder
1/2 teaspoon garlic powder
1/2 teaspoon salt
1 lb. snapper fillets cut into equal size pieces
2 medium tomatoes each cut into 4 slices
8 1 oz. slices monterey jack cheese
4 tablespoons grated parmesan cheese

Heat oven to 350˚. Melt butter in 9X13 inch baking dish. Stir in basil, onion powder, garlic powder and salt. Dip both sides of each fillet of in melted seasoned butter. Set half of the total fillets aside. Place remaining fillets in the baking dish. Layer each fillet with one tomato slice and 1 cheese slice, top with the fillets which were set aside. Secure each with a wooden toothpick. Sprinkle with parmesan cheese. Bake for 20-30 minutes or until fish flakes.

PICKLED NORTHERN

(Other fish may be substituted)

Recipe for 1 quart:

Fillets should be clean with skin and rib bones removed. Cut fillets cross grain into 1 inch strips. Loosely pack fish in quart jar, pour in 1/4 cup salt, pour in enough vinegar to cover fish. Close jar and refrigerate 5 to 6 days. Remove fish from refrigerator drain and rinse with clean water.

make brine of:
3/4 cup sugar
3/4 tablespoon pickling spice
1 1/4 cup vinegar

Heat slowly until sugar is dissolved. Cool, pack fish in clean jars alternating levels with large sliced onion. Pour in cooled brine to cover. Close jar and refrigerate. Fish can be eaten the next day.

CANNED SALMON

(For pint and half-pint jars)

Use only clean fresh fish. Cut fish into lengths 1/2 shorter than the length of the jar. Soak in brine, 1/2 cup salt to 1 gallon water, for 60 minutes, Drain well, rinse. Pack solidly in jars leaving 1/2 inch head space.

add:
1 tablespoon catsup
1 tablespoon vegetable oil
1/8 teaspoon worchestershire sauce (optional)
1/2 teaspoon salt

Wipe rim of jar with clean cloth, adjust jar lids. Process in pressure cooker at 15 pounds pressure for 90 minutes.

SNAKE RIVER STEELHEAD

The power and strength of this trophy deserves special recognition at your table.

4 fillets or steaks 1 inch thick, approx. 8-10 oz. each - steelhead or salmon
1/3 cup bourbon whiskey
1/3 cup vegetable oil
2 tablespoons soy sauce
1 teaspoon salt
1/4 teaspoon freshly ground black pepper

Preheat oven to 425°, place fillets or steaks in a 9X13 baking pan. Combine bourbon, oil, soy sauce, salt and pepper. Brush basting mixture on fillets. Bake uncovered, basting frequently for approx. 12-15 minutes or until fish flakes easily at its thickest part.

GRILLED BROOK TROUT

4 brook trout cleaned, approx 1 pound each

marinade:
1/4 cup lemon juice
2 tablespoons vegetable oil
2 tablespoons sesame seeds
1 tablespoon tabasco sauce
1/2 teaspoon ground ginger
1/2 teaspoon salt

Combine all ingredients for marinade and mix well. Place trout in a shallow baking dish and pour over marinade. Cover and refrigerate 1 hour turning several times. Remove fish from marinade, place on well greased rack and cook 4-5 inches over medium hot coals for about 5 minutes, turn, baste with existing marinade and cook an additional 5 minutes or until fish flakes easily at its thickest part.

HALIBUT IN SALSA

4 halibut steaks 1/2 lb. ea.
4 tablespoons olive oil
1 large onion chopped
1 small carrot shredded
3 ripe tomatoes, peeled, diced
6 oz. tomato juice
1 bunch fresh parsley
2 garlic cloves minced
2 tablespoons red wine vinegar
3 jalapeno peppers minced

Heat olive oil in fry pan and add onion and carrot, sauté until onion becomes transparent, add tomatoes and cook over low heat for 5 minutes. Add tomato juice, parsley, wine vinegar, garlic and peppers. Cook 3 to 5 minutes. Arrange fish fillets in casserole, pour salsa mixture over fish and bake at 350° for 20 minutes.

CAMPBELL RIVER MARINATED SALMON STEAKS

A fine way to present that trophy tyee.

4 salmon steaks about 1 inch thick
1/2 cup vegetable oil
1/2 cup dry white wine
1 teaspoon sugar
1 garlic clove minced
1 small onion minced
1/4 cup koerners or dijon style mustard
1/8 teaspoon paprika

In shallow bowl, blend all ingredients. Place salmon steaks in a zip lock plastic bag and pour marinade over fish. Seal the bag, refrigerate for approx. 2 hours turning bag several times.

Remove steaks from bag. To grill, place on a well greased rack 4-5 inches from coals for approx. 5 minutes each side, baste frequently with remaining marinade.

DEEP FRIED CATFISH
AND HUSH PUPPIES

2 lbs. catfish or bullhead fillets
1/2 cup buttermilk
1 cup yellow cornmeal
peanut oil

Heat 3-4 inches of peanut oil to 375˚ in a deep fat fryer. Dip fish in buttermilk, roll in cornmeal to coat. Fry a few pieces at a time for about 4 minutes or until they turn a deep golden brown. Drain on paper towel, keep warm until served.

HUSH PUPPIES

1 cup yellow corn meal
1/3 cup flour
1 teaspoon sugar
1 teaspoon baking powder
1/8 teaspoon salt
1/8 teaspoon seasoned salt
1 egg
1 small onion minced
1 8 oz. can cream-style corn
2 tablespoon buttermilk
peanut oil

Heat 3-4 inches of oil to 375˚. Mix dry ingredients in medium bowl, add remaining ingredients and mix lightly until combined. Drop batter into hot oil one tablespoon at a time. Fry a few at a time for 4-5 minutes or until golden brown. Drain on paper towel.

Serve hot with catfish.

MILLE LACS WALLEYE SUPREME

*When a "big one" finds its way into your creel, try this elegant
yet light way to create a really special meal.*

2 whole fillets from a 6-10 lb. walleye, or other large, light flesh fish.
1 tablespoon vegetable oil
2 stalks celery, chopped
1/2 green pepper chopped
1/2 sweet red pepper chopped
1 medium onion chopped
6 fresh mushrooms sliced
1 garlic clove minced
1 teaspoon curry powder
1 teaspoon flour
1/2 cup milk
1 cup dry white wine
1 cup cooked baby shrimp
1/2 teaspoon salt
3 tablespoons butter, melted

Sauté celery, onion, peppers, mushrooms, and garlic in the vegetable oil in heavy fry pan over medium heat, 4-6 minutes. Add curry powder, flour and milk, mix well, stir into vegetables; add wine, shrimp, salt, stir over low heat until mixture thickens. Remove from heat, set aside.

Lightly grease oven broiler pan. Place one fillet on pan, spread about half of the stuffing mixture on the fillet. Cut a slit length-wise down the lateral line of the other fillet leaving 2-3 inches uncut on each end. Place cut fillet on top of the other fillet. Spoon the remaining stuffing in the cavity made by the slit.

Bake at 325° for approx. 35-40 minutes or until both fillets flake easily at their thickest part. Baste with butter several times during the cooking process.

BROILED TROUT WITH MUSTARD SAUCE

6 fillets from 1-2 lb. trout
1/4 teaspoon salt
1/4 teaspoon freshly ground black pepper
2 tablespoons butter, melted

sauce:
1 tablespoon minced onion
1 tablespoon minced sweet red pepper
2 tablespoons butter
1 tablespoon flour
1/4 teaspoon salt
1 cup milk
2 tablespoons koerner or dijon style mustard

Melt butter in small sauce pan, lightly sauté onion and red pepper. Stir in flour, salt, slowly stir in milk, add mustard and continue to cook until thickened - approx. 4 minutes, stirring constantly.

Place fillets on broiler pan, place approx. 5 inches under broiler for 12-15 minutes. Halfway through the cooking process, baste fillets with melted butter.

Transfer fillets to serving platter, pour over sauce and serve.

BROILED STRIPPER
WITH ORANGE SAUCE

This hybrid is a superb challenge on the water, it's elusiveness is surpassed only by the ferocious battle it gives the fortunate angler.

2 lbs. fillet of striped bass
2 tablespoons butter
2 tablespoons minced onion
1 tablespoon flour
1 teaspoon orange zest
1/4 teaspoon salt
1/4 teaspoon freshly ground black pepper
1 cup milk

Begin by making orange sauce. In small saucepan melt butter over medium heat. Add onion and sauté lightly. Stir in flour, orange zest, salt and pepper. Slowly add milk stirring until thickened. Cook an additional 5 minutes.

Cut fish into serving pieces, approx. 4 in. long, place on broiler pan, place under broiler for approx. 12-18 minutes or until fish flakes at its thickest part.

Remove fish from broiler, pour sauce over, serve.

GRILLED LAKE TROUT

Lake trout or "mackinaws" tend to be oily, which taints the flesh when they are baked or fried. Grilling lakers in this manner bakes out the oil and lets it drop in the coals, away from the flesh, leaving a very delicate tasting fillet.

fillets cut from fish, leaving skin on
1/2 cup butter, melted
1/8 teaspoon garlic powder
1/2 teaspoon seasoned salt
fresh ground black pepper

Sprinkle seasoned salt on fillets. Grill fillets covered, skin side down on a well greased rack, 3-4 inches above coals for 12-18 minutes. Combine melted butter and garlic powder and baste twice during the cooking process. Fish will be done when it flakes easily at its thickest part.

Squeeze on fresh lemon juice, sprinkle freshly ground pepper, serve hot.

KETCHICAN CRAB MORNAY

Some days in life far exceed our expectations, this is one of those extraordinary experiences.

2 lbs. crab meat
4 tablespoons dry bread crumbs
3 table spoons melted butter
paprika

sauce ingredients:
2 cups whipping cream
2 cups half and half
1/4 cup flour
1/4 cup dry white wine
1/2 cup grated parmesan cheese
salt, white pepper

Combine whipping cream and half and half in large saucepan. Bring to boil taking care not to scorch. Heat butter in small skillet, stir in flour until smooth and golden. Stir in 4 tablespoons of hot cream, add to cream mixture in saucepan and bring to boil stirring constantly. Add wine and cheese and simmer over low heat until blended. Season with salt and pepper.

Spread 1/4 cup sauce in the bottom of each of 8 individual casseroles. Sprinkle 4 ounces of crab meat in each casserole, cover with 1/4 cup sauce, sprinkle with bread crumbs, drizzle with butter, sprinkle with paprika. Bake at 375° for 10 to 12 minutes.

NORTH COUNTRY WHITEFISH WITH ALMONDS

2 lbs. clean fillets of whitefish
2 eggs
1/8 cup milk
3/4 cup flour
1/2 teaspoon salt
1/4 teaspoon black pepper
1/2 teaspoon seasoned salt
6 tablespoons vegetable oil
4 tablespoons butter
1/8 cup slivered almonds
2 tablespoons lemon juice

Beat eggs and milk. Mix dry ingredients, rinse fillets and pat dry. Dip fillets in milk egg mixture and dredge in flour.

Fry over medium heat in oil with two tablespoons of butter until golden brown, turn once.

Simultaneously sauté almonds in 2 tablespoons butter until brown, remove from heat, add lemon juice. Spoon over fillets and sprinkle with parsley flakes and enjoy.

SALMON IN FOIL

Use for any salmon or large trout, including steelhead.

2 pounds salmon fillet, skin removed
2 tablespoons butter
10 medium sized fresh mushroom sliced
2 medium carrots quartered, cut in strips
1 medium zuccini, sliced and quartered
3 green onions, minced
1 sweet red pepper, chopped
1 tablespoon fresh tarragon, minced
1 teaspoon salt
1/2 teaspoon freshly ground black pepper

Melt butter in fry pan over medium heat, lightly sauté mushrooms, carrots, zuccini and pepper.

Cut fish into 4 equal pieces. Cut aluminum foil in 4 12X12 sheets. Place 1/4 of the vegetables on each sheet of foil, place a fillet on top of vegetables and sprinkle each with onion, tarragon, salt and pepper, fold and seal foil. Place on broiler pan, in oven 5-6 inches from heat for 18-25 minutes or until fish flakes easily at its thickest part.

SAVORY SEAFOOD NEWBERG

1 lb. cod, sole, snapper, or bass
1 lb. lobster, crabmeat, or scallops
4 tablespoons butter
3 tablespoons lemon juice
1 teaspoon salt
1 tablespoon flour
1/2 teaspoon paprika
1/8 teaspoon cayenne
3 cups cream
3 egg yolks
2 tablespoons sherry

Melt butter in heavy frypan over medium heat. Cut seafood into one inch pieces and lightly sauté for about 5 minutes, add lemon juice. Mix flour, salt, paprika and cayenne, add to seafood. Slowly add 2 cups of cream. Stir and bring mixture to a simmer. Combine eggs with the remaining cup of cream, blend with seafood, stir until slightly thickened. Add sherry just before serving.

Serve over rice.

BOILED GULF SHRIMP

3 lbs. fresh jumbo shrimp
2 12 oz. cans or bottles of beer
1 garlic clove, peeled
1 tablespoon salt
1 teaspoon thyme
2 bay leaves
2 tablespoons celery seed
2 tablespoons chopped parsley
1/4 teaspoon tabasco
juice from 1/2 fresh lemon

Split shrimp down the back, remove the vein and legs but leave shell on. Combine beer (water may be used in place of the beer) and seasoning. In large kettle bring to a boil, reduce heat and simmer 2-5 minutes or until shrimp turns pink.

Serve hot with drawn butter or cocktail sauce.

37

BIG GAME

North American big game, whether it be the majestic elk or moose, the fleet footed pronghorn or the popular white tail, can be transformed into delicacies worthy of any table. The rich red texture of venison is totally versatile and lends well to countless varieties of cookery. In spite of this, there are those who consider sausage the only acceptable method for preparing and eating venison. Don't get me wrong. I love sausage in its many variations. Furthermore, I'll share family recipes in this book. But, it is sacrilege to process and entire animal into ground smoked sticks.

The universal rule is: If you want good tasting venison, you must take exceptional care in the field from the moment your animal is harvested. This means being prepared, having proper equipment and a sense for the task at hand. Careful preservation will greatly enhance the quality and rich flavor of your meat.

It seems like each hunting camp has its own rituals for handling harvested game. There are advocates for bleeding, removing musk glands, hanging, aging etc.. Perhaps at some point or other each has its place and tradition is important. However, quick gutting, cleanliness and cooling is essential. In some instances this means skinning immediately. When nature permits, I like to hang the skinned animal for 5 to 7 days at temperatures near freezing.

When butchering, consider the many ways you plan to prepare your meals. The number of people in your family, and their appetites. Then cut, wrap and mark your packages accordingly. Always trim away all fat, wrap the meat tightly with quality freezer paper and try to eliminate any air pockets in the package. If you plan to share your bounty do it early, don't wait until it has been in the freezer for months.

The recipes that follow can be used with any animals considered big game if your common sense prevails. Elk, moose, caribou, and deer meat can be readily substituted. You will want to make some trial runs when substituting wild sheep, goat, boar, or even pronghorn.

Unless indicated in the recipe, venison should be served on the rare side to prevent it from being dry or tough. Quality gourmet venison will be at its tender sizzling best when served rare with little seasoning other than salt and pepper and served on hot plates.

VENISON STEAKS ON THE GRILL

1 steak cut from the loin 3/4 inch thick
2 tablespoons butter
salt and pepper

Coat top half of the steak with 1 tablespoon butter, grill steak on well greased rack 3-4 inches above the coals for 3-4 minutes. Turn steak, coat with remaining butter and grill for 2-3 minutes longer. Season to taste with salt and pepper.

This is venison at its finest, unpretentious, delicious form.

VENISON SWISS STEAK

4 steaks approx. 1/2 lb. each
1/3 cup flour
1/4 teaspoon pepper
1/8 teaspoon seasoned salt
4 tablespoons cooking oil
1/2 cup minced onion
6 fresh mushrooms sliced
1 beef bouillon cube

Mix dry ingredients and dredge each steak. Heat cooking oil over medium heat in a heavy frying pan and brown steaks. When steaks are turned add onion, mushrooms and brown. Add 2 1/2 cups water, bouillon cube, cover and simmer for one hour or until a fork can easily be withdrawn from the meat. Mixture can be thickened to desired consistency with remaining flour mixture.

Serve over hot buttered noodles, potatoes, bread or toast.

VENISON FILLET WITH CRAB SAUCE

1 venison fillet cut from saddle (about 3 lbs.)
2 tablespoons butter or margarine

Cut the fillet 3/4 - 1 inch thick. Melt butter over medium heat in large fry pan and quickly sear. Reduce heat and cook for an additional 2-3 minutes on each side. Salt, pepper lightly.

crab sauce:

Melt 1/2 cup butter in top of a double boiler, add 1 teaspoon finely minced onion. Cook gently until translucent. Add one 6 oz. can of fancy crab meat.

In separate bowl mix 1/4 cup sherry or madeira, 1 cup cream and 3 beaten egg yolks. Add to butter mixture in double boiler stirring constantly until sauce thickens.

Serve at once on hot plates, pouring the hot crab sauce over each fillet.

Serve with broccoli or brussels sprout.

VENISON STEAK PAN FRIED

1 steak cut from loin
2 tablespoons butter
salt and pepper

Melt butter in fry pan. Sear steak rapidly on both sides being cautious not to burn the butter, lower heat and cook for an additional 2-3 minutes on each side. Season to taste with salt and pepper.

For an additional treat serve with sliced onions sautéed in butter. Serve with hot crumb noodles.

VENISON MULLIGAN

Nothing tantalizes your senses like a bubbling pan of Mulligan after a full day in the field.

2 lbs. venison cut into 1 inch cubes
1/3 cup flour
1/4 teaspoon pepper
1/2 teaspoon seasoned salt
4 tablespoons cooking oil
1/2 cup minced onion
2 beef bouillon cubes
4 cups water
1 cup frozen peas
4 medium potatoes, quartered
4 carrots, sliced
2 tablespoons chopped parsley

Mix dry ingredients and dredge venison cubes. Heat cooking oil in a heavy fry pan over medium heat and brown. When pieces are turned add onion. When venison is browned add water, bouillon cubes, cover and simmer for 30 minutes. Add frozen peas, potatoe, carrots and chopped parsley. Cook approx. 30 more minutes or until everything is tender. The mixture can be thickened to the desired consistency with the remaining flour mixture. Salt to taste.

mulligan with dumplings:

To add dumplings to your already sumptuous meal, sift together 2 cups flour, 1 tablespoon baking powder, 1/2 teaspoon salt, 1/2 teaspoon seasoned salt. Cut in 1 tablespoon of butter. Add 3/4 cup of milk, mix with a folding motion.

Place batter by tablespoons full on top of the slowly bubbling mulligan. Cover and steam for 15-20 minutes.

VENISON GOULASH

3 lbs. venison shoulder cut in 1/2 inch cubes
1/3 cup flour
1/2 teaspoon seasoned salt
1/4 teaspoon black pepper
4 tablespoons cooking oil
1 cup minced onion
2 beef bouillon cubes
1 tablespoon tomato paste
1 green pepper, diced
1 1/2 cup sour cream

Mix dry ingredients and dredge meat. Heat oil in dutch oven over medium heat and brown. When pieces are turned add onions. Add 1 cup water to the tomato paste stir into meat mixture, add bouillon and green pepper. Cover and simmer until meat is tender approx. 1 1/2 hours. Stir in sour cream, simmer for an additional 2-3 minutes.

goulash with potato Dumplings:
6 medium potatoes, peeled and coarsely grated
4 slices bread with crusts trimmed.
1/2 teaspoon salt
1 medium onion, finely minced
2 eggs, beaten until frothy
1/4 cup flour

Grate potatoes and press between several layers of paper towels to remove water. Crumb bread slices and mix with grated potato, salt, onion and eggs. Shape into 1 1/2 inch balls, roll in flour, boil in water covered for approx. 12 minutes.

Serve goulash over dumplings.

43

ELK CURRY

2 lbs. elk shoulder, bone, fat, sinew removed
4 tablespoons cooking oil
2 large onions, chopped
1 garlic clove, minced
2 celery stalks, chopped
1 teaspoon worcestershire sauce
1 level tablespoon fresh curry
2 cups water
2 beef bouillon cubes

Cut meat in 1 inch cubes. Heat oil over medium heat in large fry pan. Add meat, onion, garlic and celery, stir and brown. Add worcestershire sauce, curry, water and bouillon cubes. Stir, cover and simmer for 30 minutes or until meat is tender.

Serve over rice with hot fresh bread.

VENISON STEAK IN SOUR CREAM

4 venison steaks cut from loin
4 tablespoons butter or peanut oil
1 medium onion, diced
1 cup sour cream

Melt butter over medium heat in fry pan. Brown steak on both sides. Reduce heat add onion, pour sour cream over steak. Simmer until tender stirring occasionally. Salt and pepper to taste. Sprinkle with paprika.

Serve with mashed potatoes or hot rice.

VENISON STROGANOFF

We're told this recipe dates back three generations. I can guarantee it will survive at least three more.

2 lbs. venison cut into 1 inch cubes
1/2 cup flour
1/4 teaspoon pepper
1/2 teaspoon seasoned salt
4 tablespoons cooking oil
1 clove garlic, minced
1 medium onion, chopped
1 teaspoon salt
1 beef bouillon cube
2 cups water
8 oz. fresh mushrooms sliced
1 cup sour cream

Mix flour, pepper and seasoned salt and dredge venison cubes. Heat cooking oil in heavy fry pan or dutch oven and brown meat. When pieces are turned add garlic and onion. When meat is browned add 2 cups water and mushrooms, cover and simmer for 45 minutes. Add sour cream, simmer for an additional 2 minutes.

Serve over rice, noodles or potatoes.

VENISON FAJITAS

A real Tex-Mex treat.

2 lbs. venison loin thinly sliced
1 small bottle italian dressing
2 green onions, minced
1 clove garlic, minced
1/2 teaspoon salt
1/4 teaspoon black pepper
1/4 cup worcestershire sauce
1/2 can of beer

Combine all ingredients to form marinade. Cover steak and marinate 6 hours, mixing occasionally.

Remove meat from marinade and drain. Heat 4 tablespoons cooking oil over medium heat in heavy fry pan. Quickly sear meat reduce heat, add 2 large sliced onions and simmer 8-10 minutes. Or grill over hot coals 8-10 minutes.

Slice thin and serve with traditional fixins for roll your own Tex-Mex style fajitas including flour tortillas, diced tomato, shredded lettuce, black olives, avocado slices and sour cream.

ROUGHRIDER STEW

Stews offer something for everyone. You may want to develop your own variation but, this recipe will get you started.

2 lbs. venison cut into 1 inch cubes
1 cup flour
1 teaspoon salt
1/2 teaspoon pepper
4 tablespoons butter
1 large onion, chopped
1 green pepper, chopped
2 bay leaves
3 tablespoons worcestershire sauce
4 cups water
1 stalk celery, chopped
4 medium potatoes peeled, quartered
6 carrots quartered

Mix flour salt and pepper, dredge meat. Melt butter over medium heat in heavy fry pan. Brown meat add onion, green pepper, bay leaf, and worcestershire sauce. Add water cover and simmer for 30 minutes. Add celery, potatoes and carrots and simmer for an additional 30 minutes or until vegetables are tender.

Serve with fresh baked bread.

VENISON SHOULDER ROAST

A great entree when you need to feed the crowd. The slow cooking with low heat and water keeps the meat moist.

1 venison shoulder roast 8 to 10 lbs.
1 apple, sliced
1 package dry onion soup mix
2 tablespoons worcestershire sauce
1/2 cup water
barbeque sauce

All fat should be trimmed from the roast. Season, place in roasting pan, cover with apple slices. Mix soup with water and worcestershire sauce and spread over apple slices and meat. Add an additional 1 cup water to bottom of roasting pan. Cover and cook at 250° for 6 hours. Skim off apple and soup mix. Top with your favorite barbeque sauce. Slice thin and serve.

DEEP FRIED VENISON FILLET

2 lbs. venison fillet cut 1/2 inch thick
2 cups flour
1/2 teaspoon black pepper
1 teaspoon baking powder
1/8 teaspoon garlic powder
1 cup buttermilk
1 cup water
1 teaspoon salt

Combine dry ingredients in large bowl and mix. In separate bowl combine buttermilk, water and salt and mix thoroughly. Dredge fillets in flour mixture then dip into batter, then return fillets to flour mixture and dredge. In large fry pan, dutch oven or deep fat fryer, heat oil until very hot - drop individual fillets into skillet - cook until golden brown. Serve with squash, rice or potatoes

VENISON LIVER AND ONIONS

This is a favorite in many deer camps across the country.

2 lbs. fresh venison liver
1 cup flour
1/4 teaspoon baking powder
1 teaspoon salt
1 teaspoon black pepper
1 tablespoon parsley flakes
1/3 cup vegetable oil
2 large onions, sliced
1 1/2 cups milk

Thinly slice the liver. Mix flour, baking powder, salt, pepper and parsley flakes, the dredge the liver.

Heat oil over medium heat in large fry pan. Lightly brown liver on each side. Remove liver from pan, add onions in pan and sauté until soft. Add 3 tablespoons of the flour mixture to the pan, stir and brown lightly. Add milk and stir until creamy and smooth. Return liver to pan and simmer covered over low heat 15 to 20 minutes or until liver is tender.

VENISON OSCAR

For a special dinner when elegance is required.

4 venison fillets cut from the tenderloin 1 inch thick
8 asparagus spears
8 medallions preboiled lobster or king crab meat
2 tablespoons butter

tomato sauce made from:
4 oz. white wine
1 tablespoon finely minced onion
1 tablespoon finely minced green pepper
1 tablespoon butter
1 4 oz. can tomato sauce
1/4 teaspoon salt
1/8 teaspoon black pepper

Heat asparagus in lightly salted water. Melt butter over medium heat and sauté fillets in heavy fry pan for 4-5 minutes on each side. Remove meat from pan and keep warm. Deglaze pan with white wine, add onion and green pepper. Add lobster or crab and simmer until hot. Serve meat on heated platter, top with asparagus and seafood. Pour sauce over all.

Serve with baked potato.

BADLANDS PEPPER STEAK

This mouthwatering treat will tame that big mule deer which thrives in the prairie bad lands.

2 lbs. venison round steak
1/2 cup flour
1/2 teaspoon seasoned salt
1/2 teaspoon black pepper
1 large onion, sliced
6 oz. fresh mushroom, sliced
4 teaspoons worcestershire sauce
1 large green pepper seeds removed, sliced
1 cup water

Cut steak into 1 inch strips 3 inches long. Mix flour, seasoned salt and pepper. Dredge meat. Heat oil over medium heat in large fry pan and lightly brown meat. Add onion, mushrooms and worcestershire sauce and pepper. Stir and cook for 10 minutes. Add water, cover and simmer 30 minutes or until meat is tender.

Serve with fried squash.

HOLIDAY VENISON MEATBALLS

Truly a hit at any party.

1 lb. ground venison
1 medium onion finely minced
1/4 cup milk
3/4 teaspoon salt
1/2 cup soft bread crumbs
1 cup flour
3 tablespoons cooking oil
3 tablespoons molasses
3 tablespoons vinegar
3 tablespoons prepared mustard
1/4 cup catsup

Mix meat, onion, milk, salt and bread crumbs. Shape into balls 1 inch in diameter and roll in flour. Heat cooking oil over medium heat in large fry pan and brown meatballs. Remove meatballs from pan and stir molasses, vinegar, mustard and catsup. Bring to a light boil, add meatballs and simmer 8-10 minutes.

BRANDIED VENISON FILLET

4 fillets 3/4 - 1 inch thick
2 tablespoons butter
2 tablespoons brandy
1 tablespoon worcestershire sauce

Melt butter over medium heat in large fry pan and quickly sear. Reduce heat and cook for an additional 2-3 minutes on each side. Add 2 tablespoons of butter, 2 tablespoons of brandy and 1 tablespoon worcestershire sauce. Mix together with meat and simmer for an additional minute. Serve immediately on hot plates with rice, carrots or squash.

ELK TENDERLOIN
WITH MUSHROOM SAUCE

6 fillets cut from the tenderloin 1 inch thick
1 teaspoon salt
1/2 teaspoon black pepper
4 tablespoons butter
3 cups heavy cream
6 oz. fresh mushrooms, sliced
1 small onion, minced
1/3 cup dry white wine
2 tablespoons cognac
1 cup chicken stock or bouilion

Begin by pouring 3 cups cream into a medium sized sauce pan over medium heat reduce heat when cream begins to boil and simmer stirring occasionally for 20 minutes. Cream will be reduced by one third.

Melt butter over medium heat in heavy fry pan. Sauté fillets 4-6 minutes on each side. Transfer to heated platter and keep warm. Add onions and mushrooms to the fry pan and sauté gently. Add wine and cognac and cook over medium heat for 5 minutes. Add chicken stock cook another 5 minutes reduce heat, add cream simmer 1 additional minute.

Pour sauce over fillets and serve.

SOUTHERN FRIED VENISON

2 lbs. round steak from deer, elk, antelope
1 teaspoon salt
1/2 teaspoon freshly ground black pepper
2 eggs beaten with 1 tablespoon water
1 cup finely crushed saltine cracker crumbs
1/3 cup vegetable oil
2 cups chicken stock or bouillon
1 cup fresh sliced mushrooms
1 large onion sliced
1 sweet red pepper, chopped

Pound steak well before cutting into serving pieces. Sprinkle salt and pepper on each side of meat. Dip in egg mixture, roll in cracker crumbs and lightly fry in oil in heavy fry pan over moderate heat.

Remove meat from fry pan and layer in roasting pan or dutch oven. Add mushrooms, onions, pepper and heated chicken broth. Cover and bake at 350° for 1 hour or until tender. Uncover and continue to bake until juices are absorbed.

BRAISED ELK CHOPS

4-6 elk chops, 3/4 inch thick
4 tablespoons butter
1 small onion minced
1/3 cup dry white wine
1 teaspoon basil
1 teaspoon tarragon
1/2 teaspoon salt
1/4 teaspoon black pepper

Brown meat in butter in heavy fry pan over medium heat. Transfer to large casserole. Add onion, wine, basil, tarragon salt and pepper. Bake approx. 20 minutes at 325° basting occasionally.

BARBEQUED ELK RIBS

After you've packed them off the mountains, you and your guests deserve a treat to be remembered. Elk ribs, often times discarded, can be prepared for a memorable feast with this simple yet tasty recipe.

elk ribs cut in 8 inch lengths, the quantity depends on the appetite, plan on 4 ribs per person.
barbeque sauce
2 cups ketchup
1/2 cup brown sugar
2 garlic cloves minced
2 tablespoons dry white wine
1/4 cup koerners or dijon style mustard

Steam or pressure cook ribs until tender. Let cool.

In medium size bowl combine all sauce ingredients. Place ribs in large cake pan, pour sauce over ribs and marinate overnight, turning and basting several times.

To cook, remove ribs from pan, place on grill or broiler approx. 5 inches from heat, cook, approx. 10-12 minutes, turn, baste, cook second side approx. 5 minutes, turn baste, serve and enjoy.

HEARTY ELK CAMP STEW

4 lbs. elk or other venison cut in 1 in. pieces
1 cup flour
2 teaspoons salt
1/2 teaspoon black pepper
6 tablespoons vegetable oil
5 beef bouillon cubes
5 cups water
1 cup dry, red wine
4 garlic cloves minced
2 bay leaves
3 tablespoons tomato paste
2 teaspoons dried thyme
8 carrots quartered, 1 1/2 in. long
2 large onions chopped
1 red pepper chopped
1 lb. small fresh mushrooms, cut in half
1 lb. cut green beans
3 white turnips, chopped

Mix flour, salt, pepper, dredge meat an brown in heated oil in 5-6 quart dutch oven over medium heat, browning may take 2-3 batches. When meat is browned add water, bouillon, wine, garlic, tomato paste, bay leaves and thyme. Bring to boil, immediately reduce heat to low, cover and simmer 1 hour. Add carrots, red pepper, mushrooms, green beans and turnips.

Cover and simmer an additional hour or until veggies and meat are tender. Serve over mashed potatoes or noodles.

NEW MEXICO ELK STEAK WITH NOODLES

2 lbs elk steak 1/2 inch thick, cut from loin
1/2 cup flour
1/2 teaspoon salt
1/2 teaspoon black pepper
4 tablespoons vegetable oil
1 large onion, chopped
1 red pepper, chopped
6 tablespoons chili sauce
3 tablespoons worchestershire sauce
1 1/2 cups water

Cut steak into approx. 2X2 pieces dredge in mixed flour, salt, pepper. Brown in oil in heavy fry pan over medium heat. Reduce heat, add remaining ingredients, cover and simmer for 30 minutes.

Meanwhile cook and drain 8 ounces of noodles. Toss in 3/4 cup of heated condensed cream of chicken soup.

Mound noodles, sprinkle with buttered bread crumbs and grated parmesan cheese. Serve meat over noodles.

VENISON LOIN ON A STICK

**1 1/2 lbs. loin of elk, deer or moose
cut into pieces about 2 inches square**

**marinade:
1/2 cup soy sauce
1/2 cup red rosé wine
3 cloves garlic, minced
1 tablespoon fresh ginger, minced
2 tablespoon fresh parsley, minced
1/4 teaspoon black pepper**

Mix marinade in bowl. Add meat and mix to coat, cover and refrigerate at least 6 hours.

Remove from marinade, skewer with favorite vegetables and grill 3-4 inches over hot coals on each side. Baste with marinade several times while cooking.

STUFFED ELK ROUNDSTEAK

2 lb. round steak
1/4 cup koerners german style or dijon mustard
1 cup shredded carrots
1/2 cup sweet pickles, chopped
1 medium red cabbage, shredded
1 red pepper, chopped
1/4 cup fresh parsley, chopped
1/2 cup fresh mushrooms, sliced
1 onion, chopped
1 teaspoon dried thyme
1/2 cup rosé wine
8 pieces clean string in 2 ft. lengths

Preheat oven to 350°. Pound steak until flat, brown in large heavy fry pan, remove and lay flat on top of string pieces spaced 2 in. apart.

Spread mustard on meat, sprinkle on carrots, cabbage and all other ingredients, firmly roll and tie, cutting strings at knots.

Cover and bake for 45 minutes. Remove from oven, cool slightly. Slice with very sharp knife at 1 inch intervals. Serve hot.

BITTERROOT ELK STEAK AND DUMPLINGS

2 lbs. steak cut from loin
1 cup flour
1 teaspoon black pepper
1 teaspoon salt
1 teaspoon seasoned salt
4 tablespoons vegetable oil
1 large onion chopped
1 green onion chopped
1 cup fresh mushrooms sliced
1 cup pea pods
2 cups water
2 beef bouillon cubes
2 tablespoons worchestershire sauce
1 cup sour cream

Cut steaks 3/4 in. thick, mix dry ingredients, dredge meat and brown in heavy fry pan. Add onion, pepper, and mushrooms when meat is turned. When meat is browned on both sides and onion is translucent add water, pea pods, bouillon and worchestershire, simmer for 30 minutes. Stir in sour cream. Serve over dumplings.

dumplings:

8 slices wheat bread	1 tablespoon minced onion
2 tablespoons butter	1 teaspoon salt
2 eggs	1/2 cup cracker crumbs
1 tspn chopped parsley	dash of paprika, nutmeg, ginger

Soak bread, squeeze out water and pull apart in small chunks. Melt butter in large frypan. Lightly sauté onion, add bread chunks and salt and brown lightly. Remove from heat, cool. Add eggs and cracker crumbs, parsley and spices, mix well and form into balls about 1 1/2 in. in diameter. Drop into boiling water, reduce heat and simmer for 10-12 minutes.

GRILLED SADDLE OF ELK

1 2 lb. tenderloin of elk
2 cloves fresh garlic, crushed
1 medium onion, chopped
1 medium green pepper
1 cup fresh mushrooms, sliced
1/2 teaspoon thyme crushed
2 tablespoons oil
1 14 oz. can stewed tomatoes
2 teaspoons corn starch

Rub meat with crushed garlic, broil over medium coals approx. 6 minutes per side. Simultaneously in a medium skillet cook onion, green pepper and thyme in oil over medium heat until onions are translucent. Drain tomatoes, save juice and combine with cornstarch, add tomatoes to vegetables, add juice and cook until thickened. Slice meat, top with vegetables and serve.

ELK CHILI

If mild chili is your choice, this recipe will satisfy.

2 lbs. ground elk meat
4 tablespoons vegetable oil
1 large onion, chopped
1 green pepper, chopped
1 cup fresh mushrooms, sliced
3 stalks celery, chopped
6 medium ripe tomatoes, peeled, quartered
1 medium zucchini cut into 1/2 inch cubes
1 32 oz. can V8 juice
1 16 oz. can red kidney beans
1 16 oz. can chili beans
1/2 teaspoon chili powder
1 teaspoon ground cumin
1 6 oz. can tomato paste

Brown meat in heavy fry pan over medium heat. Lightly sauté onion, pepper, celery and mushrooms. Transfer to soup kettle, add remaining ingredients and simmer approx. 2hrs.

VENISON CHILI

2 lbs. venison loin, cubed
4 tablespoons cooking oil
1 large onion, chopped
1 green pepper, chopped
1 red pepper, chopped
3 stalks of celery, chopped
1 32 oz. can peeled whole tomatoes
1 46 oz. can V8 juice
1 32 oz. can chili beans
1 16 oz. can red kidney beans
1 3 oz. can jalapeno peppers sliced
1 12 oz. can tomato paste
1 teaspoon salt
1/2 teaspoon black pepper
1 teaspoon hot chili pepper

Brown meat in heavy fry pan over medium high heat, add onion and cook until lightly brown. Transfer meat and onion to soup kettle. Add remaining ingredients and simmer covered for 2-3 hours stirring occasionally.

Serve with freshly minced raw onions and grated cheddar cheese sprinkled on top.

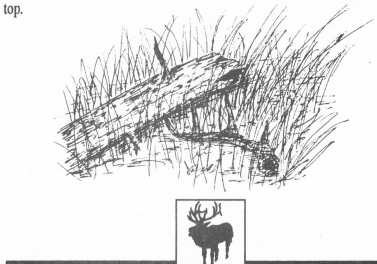

WYOMING PRONGHORN CHILI

2 lbs ground antelope or venison
1 large onion, chopped
1 green pepper, chopped
1 32 oz. can stewed tomatoes
1 46 oz. can tomato juice
1 12 oz. can tomato paste
1 32 oz. can chili beans
1 16 oz. can kidney beans
1 12 oz. can beer
1 cup black olives sliced
1/4 cup brown sugar
2 tablespoons worchestershire sauce
1 teaspoon salt
1/2 teaspoon black pepper
1 tablespoon chili powder

Brown meat in heavy fry pan over medium heat. Lightly sauté onion and green pepper. Transfer meat, onion and pepper to soup kettle, add remaining ingredients and simmer covered for 1-2 hours.

Serve with thick slices of sourdough or beer bread.

"Prairie Goat"

Michael
Thomas
Burch
C'90

65

"The Farmlander"
4-83

Michael
Thomas
Kinch

SAUSAGE AND JERKY

Maintaining adequate protein in the human diet is essential to good health. Meat and fish is an available source of protein and has always been an integral staple in the North American diet. However, without refrigeration fresh meat will spoil quickly. Therefore it is interesting to see how different cultures responded or created methods of meat preservation that withstood time and climate.

Pemmican, jerky, sausage and squaw candy are all examples or products of early processing using smoke or drying. These processes would yield a nutritious yet light weight product because, most of the water had been removed. These products sustained many settlers, adventurers, trappers and miners as they worked to extract a life from the land.

Many of these same products exist today. Processing has taken on a whole new dimension in commercial food preparation and you can purchase a variety of preserved products in any supermarket. Fortunately, some of these recipes and processes have withstood technology and fast food mania and enable us to practice this art in the tradition of our forefathers in our homes.

One such tradition is practiced each fall in the homestead of my Grandfather where the fifth generation of Euro-Americans had taken residence. There, in central Wisconsin, the act of sausage making means "home made". From the butchering to the tasting, this family activity and recipe has sustained time with new generations replacing the old in traditional chores.

While I have received, tasted, and enjoyed countless variations of sausage, I have found none to equal the coarse textured, rich moist product created by Grandpa Borchardt. It took some persuading, even a promise or two, but in this chapter I am pleased to share my Grandfather's sausage recipes.

67

GRAMPA BORCHARDTS' VENISON SUMMER SAUSAGE

To make 100 pounds of sausage, this recipe will serve you with outstanding results. It's my family's favorite.

30 lbs. venison, all fat removed
30 lbs. lean pork
40 lbs. beef

1 1/2 cups black pepper
2 1/2 cups canning salt
2 1/4 cups brown sugar
12 oz. mustard seed
3 oz. paprika
3 oz. pickle freeze

Cut meat in chunks and mix together, sprinkle all seasonings over meat and mix thoroughly. Run through a meat grinder on coarse grind, then repeat on fine grind.

For best results, stuff in cleaned, natural hog casings. Using string, tie off at each end.

the smoking process:
Use hardwood, preferably hickory, apple. Using cool smoke, 80°-95° will require a longer smoking process, 7-12 days. A hot smoke will certainly speed up the process however, the fat and moisture will drip from the casing and your finished product may be too dry.

PEMMICAN

This is an old "trail favorite" of the early inhabitants of this country.

1 pound jerky
1 pound raw beef fat
3 tablespoons brown sugar
1/2 cup raisins

Pound the jerky into small pieces with a meat hammer or shave into pieces with a knife.

In large frypan over moderate heat, render the beef fat (do this outdoors if possible) do not boil or burn the fat. Place jerky bits in cake pan, pour hot, melted fat over jerky and mix to a sausage like consistency, add brown sugar and raisins, mix, press down to flatten in pan, cool, slice into squares, store in plastic bags in a cool place.

Pemmican is very versatile, it will last weeks without refrigeration and can be eaten raw, fried or simmered in water.

CREEKSIDE FARMS
SUMMER SAUSAGE

This recipe will yield a moist, tasty product worthy of any table or occasion.

25 lbs. venison, all fat removed
25 lbs. lean pork

1 cup black pepper
1 1/4 cup canning salt
1 cup brown sugar
4 1/2 oz. mustard seed
1 1/2 oz. paprika
1/4 cup pickle freeze

Cut meat in chunks and mix together, sprinkle all seasonings over meat and mix thoroughly. Run through a meat grinder on coarse grind, repeat on fine grind.

For best results, stuff in cleaned natural hog casings. Using string, tie off securely at each end.

the smoking process:
Use a cool smoke from a hardwood of hickory or apple with a temperature of 80°-90° for 7-12 days. The actual length of time depends on individual preference, taste and color of your sausage. I prefer a light pink center resulting in a soft moist product.

VENISON JERKY

hind quarter of venison, deboned
brine: per 1 gallon
2 pounds salt
1 teaspoon nitrate cure
1 gallon water

Debone the quarter separating the individual muscles. Using a syringe, inject brine into each muscle in several places. Place meat in a plastic pail or tub, cover with brine, weight meat down to keep it submerged. Refrigerate at 40° for 10 days.

Remove from brine, rinse, smoke at 150° for approx. 5 hrs.

Hang at 50°-68° for 2 weeks. Slice thin and enjoy.

"Blackfoot Bighorn"

OVEN JERKY

6 pounds ground venison
3 tablespoons salt
1 tablespoon sugar
1 teaspoon black pepper
1 teaspoon cayenne

Sprinkle all seasoning on meat and thoroughly mix. Transfer to a well greased cake pan, place in refrigerator for 10-12 hrs. - slightly frozen meat slices better. Slice meat 1/8 in. thick, place on well greased oven rack.

mix: **1 cup warm water**
            1 teaspoon garlic powder
            2 teaspoons liquid smoke

Place ingredients in plastic spray bottle shake to mix thoroughly. Spray garlic and smoke solution on top and bottom of meat strips.

Place in 115° oven for 3 hours increase temperature to 150°, bake for additional 15 minutes then remove from oven and allow to cool to room temperature. Pack jerky in plastic bags - product will keep for months if kept cool.

"Once in a Lifetime"

Michael Thomas Burch
3-17-89
©

UPLAND GAME

Gamebirds flourish throughout our land. Although populations tend to be cyclical, habitat is probably the single most influential factor in determining numbers.

Imports and transplants have created many new opportunities for gunning and feasting. As such, the pheasant reigns supreme both in the field and on the table. This isn't meant to diminish the contribution made by chukkars, doves, quail, grouse and partridge, they provide untold opportunities and pleasure. However, few experiences afield can offer satisfaction equal to outsmarting a sassy old rooster late in the season. Gamebirds can be used in the creation of countless recipes from fancy roasting to gumbo. Their versatility offers something for everyone and they are fun to work with.

When preparing fowl it is advantageous for the cook to know the age of birds. Young birds can be prepared in any manner from charbroiling to stir-fry with great results. Old birds which tend to be stringy and tough need to be tamed. A pheasants age can be determined by the length and condition of the leg spurs. Old ringnecks will have sharp pointed spurs that are long and glossy. Young birds will have spurs that are light, dull colored and stubby. Wing tips reveal the age of grouse and partridge. On young birds the two outer most feathers will be pointed. On turkeys it is the tail feathers that tell the age. When the tail is fanned and all the feathers are even you have an old bird. However if the two center feathers are longer the bird is a young one. As with all game proper care in the field is essential to quality eating. Birds should be drawn as quickly after downing as possible. Upon arrival home the birds should be hung in a cool place at less than 40° for 2 days before cleaning. When freezing, you will do well to mark the species, condition and age of your bird on the package. This will definitely help when considering your recipe options.

ROAST PHEASANT

1 young 2-3 lb. pheasant
1 bay leaf
2-3 tops from celery stalks
1 medium onion, quartered
1 lemon slice
4 tablespoons butter
1 cup chicken stock
6 oz. fresh mushrooms sliced

Rinse bird, pat dry with paper towel. Lightly rub inside and out with salt, pepper and butter. Place bay leaf, celery tops, onion and lemon inside cavity. Put bird on rack in roasting pan with breast down. Pour in chicken stock and mushrooms.

Cover and roast at 350° for approx. 1 1/2 hours basting every 15 minutes. To brown bird, remove cover during last 15 minutes of cooking time. Gravy can be made from pan drippings.

Serve with squash, potato or rice.

BREAST OF PHEASANT WITH STUFFING

With good friends and good wine, life has offered its best.

4 boned breast halves (use young pheasants only)
1 stick butter
1 pound fresh mushrooms sliced
1 medium onion, minced
1 stalk celery, minced
6 slices wheat bread, finely cubed
3 tablespoons cream
1/2 cup chicken stock
1 can cream of mushroom soup
1/2 can milk
2 tablespoons sherry

Melt 1/2 stick butter over medium heat in heavy fry pan. Add mushrooms, onion and celery. Sauté lightly for 3-5 minutes or until onions are translucent. Add bread cubes and stir over heat until lightly brown. Add cream, salt and pepper to taste.

Remove stuffing from pan. Melt remaining 1/2 stick butter over medium heat. Sauté pheasant breast until lightly browned (4-6 minutes) return stuffing to fry pan, pour in stock, cover and simmer for 20 minutes. Heat soup and milk and stir in sherry. Arrange pheasant and stuffing on individual warmed plates, pour on sherry mushroom sauce.

PHEASANT STROGANOFF

(Peckerwood Stew)

2 pheasants boned, cut in bite size chunks
1 cup flour
1/2 teaspoon salt
1/2 teaspoon black pepper
1/2 teaspoon seasoned salt
4 tablespoons cooking oil
1 large onion, chopped
8 fresh mushrooms, sliced
2 celery stalks, chopped
1 can cream of celery soup
1 can cream of mushroom soup
1 cup milk
1/4 cup sherry

Combine flour, salt, pepper, seasoned salt and dredge pheasant chunks. Heat cooking oil in heavy fry pan or dutch oven and brown meat. Drain off excess cooking oil. Add celery and onion and sauté lightly. Add mushroom soup, celery soup and milk, stir briefly. Cover and simmer on lowest heat for 2-3 hours stirring occasionally. Add sherry 15 minutes before serving.

In the meantime cook enough rice preferably a combination of long grain and wild rice and serve the pheasant over the rice.

PHEASANT REMINGTON

1 pheasant
1 medium onion, chopped
1/4 cup olive oil
1 16 oz. whole canned tomatoes
1 teaspoon salt
1/4 teaspoon black pepper
2 cups red california burgundy
1/4 teaspoon orange zest
1/4 teaspoon sweet basil, crushed
6 oz. fresh mushrooms, sliced

Cut pheasant into serving pieces. Cover with cold lightly salted water, refrigerate for 2 hours; drain well. Heat olive oil in dutch oven over medium heat and lightly brown the onion. Add tomatoes, salt, pepper and pheasant. Cook uncovered in 350° oven for 1 hour. Add burgundy, seasonings, and mushrooms. Cover and continue cooking at 350° for another hour.

Serve with choice of potato or rice.

PHEASANT SOUP

Many of the recipes for pheasant call for only the breast meat, and to waste the rest of the carcass is practically unthinkable. Therefore, save those remaining parts and use them to create a delicate broth from which you can create your best soup ever.

carcasses from 2 pheasants
4 quarts water
1 teaspoon salt
1 stalk celery, minced
2 carrots, minced
4-6 chicken bouillon cubes
1 cup rice

egg drops:
4 eggs, beaten
1 1/2 cups flour
1/4 teaspoon baking powder
1/2 teaspoon salt
1 teaspoon parsley flakes

Clean and rinse pheasants, place in soup pot with water and salt. Boil covered over medium heat for 30 minutes, remove from heat, skim froth from broth, clean meat from bones. Add meat, celery, carrots, bouillon, rice, cover and simmer 30-45 minutes.

Make egg drops by beating 4 eggs til frothy, add other ingredients, mix well. Batter should be stiff, add more flour if necessary. Drop by the spoonful in broth. Simmer 10-12 minutes.

PHEASANT WINCHESTER

2 young pheasants quartered, cut in serving pieces
1/2 cup flour
1/2 teaspoon seasoned salt
1/4 teaspoon black pepper
4 tablespoons butter
1 medium onion, minced
4 carrots, quartered
1 teaspoon thyme
1 pint cream
1 cup water
paprika

Mix flour, seasoned salt and pepper. Dredge pheasant pieces. Melt butter over medium heat in heavy fry pan and gently brown. Transfer the browned meat to a small roaster or dutch oven. Add onion, carrots and sprinkle with thyme. Add the cream and water, cover and roast at 350° for 1 hour.

Serve with hot baking powder biscuits.

BRAISED PHEASANT LEGS

6-8 pheasant legs or thighs
1 can beer
1/2 cup flour
1/2 teaspoon seasoned salt
1/4 teaspoon black pepper
3 tablespoons cooking oil
1 medium onion, chopped
1 chicken bouillon cube
6 fresh mushrooms sliced

Marinate the legs in beer for 4-6 hours turning occasionally. Mix flour, seasoned salt and pepper and dredge meat. Heat cooking oil over medium heat in fry pan and brown the legs and chopped onion. Add 1 cup beer from the marinade and the bouillon cube and mushrooms. Cover and simmer for 1 1/2 hours or until legs are tender.

PHEASANT CIDER STEW

When the old rooster has a long tail, dark legs and hooked spurs, try this simple recipe to tame the meat.

1 old pheasant, disjointed
1/4 cup butter
3 apples peeled, core removed and quartered
2 teaspoons cinnamon
2 cups apple cider

Melt butter over medium heat in dutch oven, or fry pan if you later transfer the meat to a crock pot. Brown meat on both sides. Add remaining ingredients, cover, simmer until pheasant is tender. Serve with Dakota bread

SAUTEED PHEASANT CHUNKS
(Appetizer)

2 skinned and filleted pheasant breasts
3 tablespoons butter
1 small onion, minced
1/3 cup dry vermouth

    Cut meat into bite size pieces. Melt butter over medium heat in large fry pan. Quickly sauté the meat and onion for 3-4 minutes. Add vermouth and continually stir meat in wine for 1 minute. Serve hot.

WILD GIBLETS IN WINE SAUCE
(Appetizer)

1 lb. giblets, heart, gizzard, livers, from any game birds.
3 tablespoons butter
2 tablespoons flour
1/2 teaspoon salt
1 cup dry white wine
2 cups chicken stock

    Parboil giblets in lightly salted water for 10 minutes, drain and rinse. Melt butter over medium heat in large fry pan cut giblets into bite size pieces dredge in flour and sauté until browned. Mix wine and chicken stock, pour over giblets, cover and simmer for 30-40 minutes stirring occasionally. Serve as an appetizer with toothpicks.

PHEASANT WEATHERBY

This recipe enjoys a delicious blend of two different but distinct cultures.

2 pheasants cut in serving pieces
1 bottle of champagne
1 large onion, minced
2 carrots, thinly sliced
1 stalk celery, thinly sliced
1/2 teaspoon seasoned salt
1/4 teaspoon black pepper
4 tablespoons butter
1 oz. brandy
1/2 pint cream

Combine 1/2 the champagne, onion, carrot, celery, seasoned salt, and pepper. Marinate pheasant pieces for 24 hours. Remove heat in heavy fry pan or dutch oven. Sauté meat until light brown. Add marinade, cover and simmer for 30 minutes. Pour in brandy, add remaining champagne and simmer for 30 minutes uncovered. Transfer meat to platter, keep warm. Stir in cream and simmer, thicken to desired consistency with flour or cornstarch paste.

Serve over Indian Fried Bread▶

INDIAN FRIED BREAD

2 cups flour
1/3 cup dry powdered milk
2 teaspoons baking powder
1 teaspoon salt
1 tablespoon shortening
3/4 cup warm water

Measure dry ingredients into deep mixing bowl. Add shortening and work with hands until absorbed by flour. Add warm water and knead with hands until dough is smooth and does not stick to the side of the bowl (at least 5 minutes). Cover with cloth and set in a warm place and let rest for 45-60 minutes.

Heat enough vegetable oil in deep fry pan to achieve 1 inch in depth. Heat to 375°, a small piece of dough when placed in oil will rise immediately to the surface. Or a test the Indians use is to drop a match into the oil, when it ignites the oil is ready.

Tear off pieces of dough approx. the size of a racquet ball. On a floured surface with a floured rolling pin, roll each ball into a circle 1/4 inch thick. (Circle will be 6-8 inches in diameter.) Place circles in the hot oil, fry to a golden brown, turn only once.

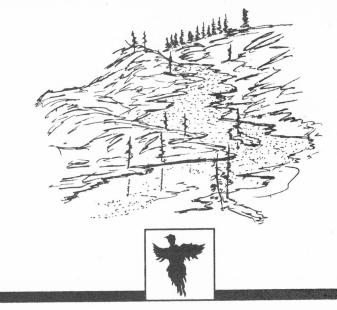

CAMPFIRE GROUSE

When you're the camp cook and the gunning has been good,
this simple, tasty recipe will forge bonds that could last forever.

1 bird per person
1 1/2 tablespoons butter
1/2 teaspoon salt
1/4 teaspoon black pepper

Split birds down the middle, rub well with butter, salt and pepper. Broil over glowing coals for about 8 minutes per side or until done to your taste. Serve with roast onions made by cross slicing a medium onion 1/2 way through, dab on 1 teaspoon butter a little seasoned salt, roll in aluminum foil and toss in the coals for 6-8 minutes.

Coal baked potatoes and sweet corn should also accompany this meal.

BREAST OF GROUSE

A delicious creation suitable for preparing any member of the grouse family.

breasts from 3 grouse
1/2 cup flour
1/2 teaspoon seasoned salt
1/4 teaspoon black pepper
4 tablespoons butter
1 medium onion, minced
6 oz. fresh mushrooms, sliced
1 pint cream
1/4 cup cooking sherry
2 tablespoons corn starch
2 cups rice

Mix flour, seasoned salt and pepper, dredge breasts, melt butter over medium heat in heavy fry pan, lightly brown the breast and onion. Add the mushrooms. Cover and simmer for 20 minutes or until a fork can easily pierce the meat.

Simultaneously cook 2 cups of rice according to directions on the package. In a separate pan heat the cream and sherry (do not boil), thicken by slowly stirring in a premoistened cornstarch paste.

Spread the rice in a large pan, nestle the grouse breasts in the rice. Spoon on the mushrooms, pour sauce over your creation, sprinkle with parmesan cheese and brown under the broiler.

NEW ENGLAND PARTRIDGE

This inhabitant of our woodlands and forests offers a supreme challenge and delectable dining.

1 ruffed grouse, picked, skin on
3 tablespoons butter
1 large bunch grapes
1 apple, sliced
1 oz. brandy
1/2 pint cream

Melt butter over medium heat in dutch oven. Brown the bird, lightly salt and pepper. Stuff the cavity of the bird with grapes and apple, add remaining grapes around the bird in the dutch oven. Cover the bird if you have enough grapes. Cover the dutch oven and roast at 375° for 30 minutes. About 5 minutes before you remove the bird from the oven, pour the brandy over it. Remove bird from dutch oven, warm. Skim the grapes from the drippings, stir in cream.

Serve with potato, rice, squash or thick toast.

DOVE CASSEROLE

breast fillets from 8-12 doves
1/2 cup flour
1/2 teaspoon seasoned salt
1/4 teaspoon black pepper
4 tablespoons butter
1 small can mushrooms, sliced
1 stalk celery, minced
1 tablespoons orange zest
2 cups dry white wine

Mix flour, seasoned salt and pepper. Dredge breast fillets. Melt butter over medium heat in large fry pan, sauté breast until golden brown. Place breast fillets in a casserole large enough to allow a single layer.

Sprinkle with mushrooms, celery and orange zest over fillets, pour in wine. Cover and bake at 325° for 30 minutes or until tender.

Serve with steamed carrots and broccoli.

HUNS

breast fillets from 6-8 hungarian partridge
1 cup flour
1 teaspoon salt
1/2 teaspoon black pepper
4 tablespoons butter
2 green onions, minced
1/2 cup cooking sherry
2 cans chicken noodle soup

Mix flour, salt and pepper. Dredge breast fillets. Melt butter over medium heat in large fry pan. Lightly brown fillets on all sides. Add onion, sherry and soup, cover and simmer for 30 minutes or until meat is tender.

Serve with your favorite potato or rice.

TURKEY CASSEROLE

Any upland bird could be used in this delicious dish.

4 cups left over turkey meat
10 oz. frozen peas
1 can cream of mushroom soup
1 can evaporated milk
4 cups seasoned croutons
1 cup butter or margarine

Mix meat, peas, mushroom soup and evaporated milk. Pour into a 9X13 lightly greased pan. Mix croutons with 1 cup melted butter, pour over the turkey mixture. Bake at 350 for 35-40 minutes.

ROAST TURKEY

Roast turkey is as old as this country. If your trophy is an old tom, you should use the recipe for steam roasted giant honker. If your bird is young this recipe will do nicely.

1 young 8-10 lb. bird
6 tablespoons butter
1 large onion, minced
2 stalks celery, minced
6 oz. fresh mushrooms, sliced
6 slices whole wheat bread, toasted, cubed
3/4 teaspoon salt
1/4 teaspoon pepper
1/2 teaspoon poultry seasoning
1 teaspoon dried sage leaves or 1/2 teaspoon dried sage
1 cup water

Rinse and dry turkey inside and out. Pull off any loose fat. Cut off the wings at the elbow.

Melt butter over medium heat in large fry pan. Sauté onion, celery, and mushrooms until lightly browned. Stir in bread cubes and seasonings, mix well. Remove from heat, cool for 5 minutes. Loosley fill cavity and neck with stuffing, close with skewers and string. Place on rack in roaster breast side down. Pour in 1 cup water, cover and roast at 325° for 20-25 minutes perpound.

After the initial 2 hours of roasting, baste every 15 to 20 minutes. Remove cover during the last 30 minutes and baste at 10 minute intervals. Make gravy using pan drippings. Thicken with a paste made from flour or cornstarch.

SAGE HEN SIMMERED IN WHITE WINE

2 sage hens, skinned, quartered
3 medium carrots
1 large onion, chopped
6 stalks celery
1 teaspoon salt
1/4 teaspoon freshly ground black pepper
1/4 teaspoon dried tarragon
1 bay leaf
1 1/2 cups dry white wine
1 1/2 cups clear chicken broth or bouillon

Cut the vegetables into 1 1/2 inch julienne, layer vegetables and meat in a dutch oven or large deep casserole, sprinkle in salt, pepper, tarragon and bay leaf. Pour in the wine and chicken broth. Simmer for 1 hour or until meat is tender. Remove from heat, skim fat, cover and let meat steep in the juice for 10 to 15 minutes before serving.

Serve over a bed of rice, basted with the cooking juices.

CHUKAR AND WILD RICE

4 chukar partridge, whole
3 tablespoons butter
1 onion, sliced
6 fresh mushrooms, sliced
1 sweet red pepper, sliced
1 teaspoon worchestershire sauce
1/2 teaspoon salt
1 cup sour cream

Truss the birds with string, melt butter in heavy fry pan over moderate heat, brown the birds. Remove from fry pan and place in deep covered baking dish or casserole. Lightly sauté onion, mushrooms and pepper in the same pan used for browning. Add worchestershire sauce, salt and sour cream, heat 2-3 minutes stirring constantly, pour over birds, cover and bake at 350° for 1 hour.

Serve baked birds over a bed of a mixture of long grain and wild rice. Serve sauce over birds and rice.

RUFFED GROUSE ROYALE

*After a golden day in the forest, this superb presentation of
your elusive quarry will guarantee total satisfaction.*

breast fillets from 4-6 grouse or pheasants
1/2 cup flour
1 teaspoon salt
1 teaspoon seasoned salt
1 teaspoon paprika
1/4 cup butter
2 teaspoons cornstarch
1 1/2 cups half & half
1/4 cup sherry
1 teaspoon grated lemon zest
1 tablespoon lemon juice
1/2 cup swiss cheese, shredded

Combine flour, salt, paprika and seasoned salt. Dredge meat and lightly brown
in butter in large fry pan over medium heat. Remove meat from fry pan and place in
a 9X13 baking dish. Mix corn starch with 1/2 cup of the half and half and stir into the
pan drippings. Cook over low heat and slowly stir in remaining half and half, lemon
zest, lemon juice and sherry, cook about 10 minutes or until mixture thickens. Pour
the mixture over the meat. Cover and bake at 350° for 35 min., uncover and sprinkle
on cheese, bake an additional 5 minutes.

CHAR-BROILED QUAIL

2 quail skinned, split down the back
1/3 cup red wine vinegar
1 tablespoon corn oil
1 bay leaf crumbled
1/2 teaspoon dried thyme
1/4 teaspoon freshly ground black pepper
4 strips orange peel
2 tablespooons butter
1/4 teaspoon garlic powder

Place quail in baking dish. Prepare a marinade by combining the red wine, corn oil, bay leaf, thyme, pepper and orange peel, pour mixture over birds, cover and refrigerate 2-4 hours, turning birds occasionally.

Melt butter, mix well with garlic powder. Remove birds from marinade, baste with the garlic butter.

Place on covered grill bone side down, 4-5 inches over moderately hot coals for 10-12 minutes, turn, baste and broil for an additional 8-10 minutes or until nicely browned.

Serve with fresh steamed vegetables and rice.

SMALL GAME

With all of the attention placed on pursuit of big game, trophy fish and exotic birds, it may be difficult to comprehend excitement over small game. The fact is rabbits and squirrels are the most sought after game in North America. They provide unparalleled excitement and challenge.

If the memory of your last pursuit takes you back to your childhood, you may be wise to renew your bonds with the little creatures. After all, weren't these the guys who first sharpened your senses, filled your game bag and scented the kitchen with your first wild bounty. Those were the simpler times, we would all be wise to re-live those moments one more time.

Both rabbit and squirrel have fine textured meat with little if any of the flavor generally associated with wild game. On many occasions each are substituted for chicken and even the most discriminating palate plays hard to tell the difference.

While raccoons are hunted and enjoyed throughout the country, opossums are generally associated with the south. Both animals have a porklike flavor and make excellent eating. The fat of each should be trimmed prior to cooking.

Beaver, woodchuck, and marsh rabbit, are also considered small game and enjoyed by many hunters and their families. All small game should be drawn as soon as possible and skinned by the end of the day. Rinse the meat with cool water prior to freezing and storage.

RABBIT STEW

2 rabbits cut in serving pieces
2 teaspoons salt
1/4 teaspoon black pepper
3 tablespoons butter
2 medium potatoes, quartered
1 stalk celery, chopped
2 carrots, quartered in strips
1 medium onion, chopped
2 carrots, quartered in strips
1 medium onion, chopped
1 8 oz. can tomato sauce
1 tablespoon parsley flakes

Boil rabbits in salt water for 10 minutes. Remove rabbit discard water. Again cover rabbit with salted water and simmer until rabbit is tender. Retain 2 cups of broth. Remove rabbit, drain and cool. Remove meat from bone cut into bite size pieces.

Melt butter over medium heat in dutch oven and add vegetables. Cover and cook for 15 minutes. Add broth and tomatoe sauce. Bring to a boil add rabbit, parsley, and salt to taste. Thicken to desired consistency with flour or cornstarch paste. Cook additional 15 minutes.

FRIED RABBIT

2 rabbits, cut in serving pieces
1 cup milk
1 cup flour
1/2 teaspoon seasoned salt
1/2 teaspoon black pepper
4 tablespoons butter
1 cup water
1 tablespoon parsley flakes
1/2 teaspoon paprika

Mix flour, seasoned salt and pepper. Dip rabbit pieces in milk the dredge in flour. Melt butter over medium heat in large fry pan. Fry meat till brown on each side. Stir in 2 tablespoons of the flour mixture. Add remaining milk and 1 cup water. Stir and simmer over low heat for 10-15 minutes. Sprinkle with parsley flakes and paprika.

BAKED RABBIT

2 rabbits, cut in serving pieces
2 eggs beaten till frothy
1/2 teaspoon salt
1/4 teaspoon black pepper
1 cup fine dry bread crumbs
4 tablespoons butter
2 cups chicken broth or bouillon
10 fresh mushrooms, sliced
6 small onions
1 tablespoon parsley flakes

Dip meat in egg and roll in bread crumbs. Melt butter over medium heat in large fry pan and brown the meat on each side. Transfer meat to a shallow baking dish. Pour in broth, add onions and parsley. Cover and bake at 350° for 1 hour.

SQUIRREL GUMBO

2 young squirrels, cut in serving pieces
4 tablespoons cooking oil
1 medium onion, chopped
2 stalks celery, chopped
1 green pepper, seeded, chopped
2 tablespoons parsley, chopped
1 medium carrot, sliced
1 1/2 cups fresh okra, sliced
1 quart chicken broth or bouillon
2 large tomatoes peeled, sliced
1/2 cup minute rice
2 tablespoons quick cooking tapioca

Heat oil over medium heat in a dutch oven, brown meat. Add onion, celery, green pepper, stir and cook until soft. Add fresh okra, parsley and chicken broth. Cover and simmer 45 minutes or until meat is tender. Add tomatoes, rice and quick cooking tapioca. Simmer 12 minutes.

SMOKEY MOUNTAIN FRIED SQUIRREL

2 young squirrels, cut in serving pieces
1/2 cup flour
1/2 teaspoon seasoned salt
1/4 teaspoon black pepper
4 tablespoons cooking oil
1/2 cup water
1 medium onion, chopped
3 carrots, quartered

Mix flour, seasoned salt and pepper, dredge meat. Heat cooking oil over medium heat in dutch oven. Fry meat until golden brown. Reduce heat, add water, onion and carrots. Cover and simmer 40 minutes.

BROILED SQUIRREL OR RABBIT

2 young squirrels, cut in serving pieces
1 small onion, minced
1/2 cup cooking oil
1/4 cup port wine
2 tablespoons fresh parsley, chopped
1/8 teaspoon tarragon
1/4 teaspoon black pepper

Make a marinade of onion, cooking oil, wine, parsley and sesonings. Place meat in a plastic container, pour over marinade and refrigerate at least 6 hours. Stir occasionally. Remove meat from marinade, drain, do not rinse. Place bone side down on grill over glowing charcoal. Cook approx. 15 minutes on first side, 10 minutes on the other. Baste occasinally with the marinade.

ROAST RACCOON

1 4-5 lb. raccoon, trimmed of fat
4 large apples, quartered
2 cups water
3 chicken bouillon cubes
2 large onions, chopped
2 sprigs parsley
1 teaspoon salt
1/2 teaspoon freshly ground black pepper

If your coon is an old one you will want to parboil it first in salted water for about a half hour. Place apples in the body cavity and skewer shut. Place in a roasting pan, add the chicken broth made from water and dissolved bouillon, sprinkle onions over meat, add salt, pepper. Cover and roast in oven at 325° for about 2 1/2 hours or until tender, baste occasionally during the cooking process. Remove meat from pan. Skim fat and thicken for gravy. Serve with roast sweet corn or sweet potatoes.

SMALL GAME STEW

When you need several critters to make a meal, this recipe will blend nicely.

2 lbs of rabbit, squirrel and or game birds, cut in serving pieces
4 tablespoons butter
1 large onion, chopped
1 stalk celery, chopped
1 green pepper, chopped
1 clove garlic, crushed
4 cups water
2 cubes, chicken bouillon
1/2 cup wild rice
1 cup baby carrots
6 small, whole, new potatoes

Melt butter in a large dutch oven or kettle over medium/high heat. Brown meat. Add onion, garlic, celery, pepper and lightly brown. Add water, bouillon and rice, cover and simmer for 30-40 minutes. Remove meat from kettle and take out bones. Return meat to kettle, add carrots, potatoes and peas. Simmer for an additional 30 minutes or until veggies are done. Stew may be thickened with flour or cornstarch to achieve the desired consistency.

Serve with hot sourdough or french bread.

WATERFOWL

Ducks and geese not only provide sensational gunning, but hunting them provides unequalled opportunity for camaraderie and friendship. Many bonds have been developed between father and son while patiently waiting in the blind over a spread of decoys. When the wind bites, the sleet stings, and the rush of wings fills the air, you know you are having fun.

Waterfowl also provide sensational dining. Geese are delicious and the rich dark meat of large northern ducks is a real delicacy. Diet generally determines the flavor of ducks. If your game bag includes shallow water puddle ducks from sloughs, it is best to fillet out the breasts and use only that portion of the bird. However if your bag contains big northern mallards and canvasback, you may want to dine on the entire bird.

Geese feed primarily on grain, green grasses and the green shoots from sprouted grain. Their rich dark meat is a natural delicacy and is a favored prize among many hunters and their families.

Both ducks and geese should be drawn as soon after the kill as possible. This will deter spoiling and improve the flavor of an otherwise marginal tasting bird. Unfortunately, mention of the word "duck" will send many cooks into a quandary. The age old argument of rare versus well done is still debated today. Regardless of your preferences your main objective should be variety. Cooking should be anything but boring and if a particular bird creates a challenge, then use your imagination, create something different. Enjoyment is ours for the seeking.

STEAM ROASTED GIANT HONKER

This trophy deserves the time and effort for a truly magnificent feast.

1 large goose plucked, dressed, cleaned
juice from 1 fresh lemon
salt

stuffing:

2 medium onions, minced	3 stalks celery, minced
4 tablespoons butter	1 teaspoon salt
10 fresh mushrooms, sliced	3 cups croutons
1/2 teaspoon pepper	1/4 teaspoon all spice
1/2 cup port wine	

Clean all loose fat from inside the bird. Cut off wing tips at elbow, cut off neck close to body, cut off tail. With fork or sharp knife prick skin at the base of each wing, the backs of the legs and where thigh meets back. This will prevent accumulation of melted fat. Rub bird inside and out with lemon juice and lightly salt the cavity. Place the bird on rack in roaster pan breast side up. Add 1 inch of water to the pan, place on top of stove, bring to boil, reduce heat, cover and steam for 1 hour. Add more water if necessary, do not burn dry.

To make the stuffing melt butter in heavy fry pan over medium heat, lightly sauté onion and celery, add mushrooms. Stir in croutons, salt, pepper, and all spice. Pour wine over and mix gently, remove heat.

Preheat oven to 325°, remove goose from roaster and let cool 15-20 minutes, discard the liquid from the bottom of the pan. Loosely fill the cavity of the goose with stuffing, use skewers and string to close opening, replace goose on rack in roasting pan. Add 2 cups fresh water and roast covered 2-3 hours depending on size of bird. After 1 1/2 hours baste bird every 15 minutes and remove cover for the final 30 minutes to brown. Make gravy from the pan drippings, and let your creativity flow as you prepare the rest of the meal to compliment this noble bird.

BREAST OF BLUEBILL

Breast fillets from 6-8 scaup or other small to medium size ducks.

marinade:
1 pint red wine
1 pint cold water
1 large onion, minced
1/2 teaspoon pepper
1 tablespoon salt

sauce:
1 pint red wine
1 pint cold water
3 onions, sliced
1 can whole tomatoes
1 large can sliced mushrooms including juice
1 green pepper, chopped
2 celery stalks, chopped
1 teaspoon salt
1 teaspoon seasoned salt
1/2 teaspoon pepper

Marinate the breasts 24 hours in a plastic container, refrigerate, stir occasionally. Remove from marinade, drain well, do not rinse.

Mix together the ingredients for the sauce in a dutch oven or soup pot. Add the duck breasts and simmer for 1 hour or until breasts are tender.

Serve with thick sliced beer bread.

MALLARD BREASTS IN WINE

Each fall we await the rapid wing beat of the great northern mallards as they migrate south. Each fall we dine on the rich red meat of this remarkable bird.

breast fillets from 2 mallards
4 tablespoons butter
1/3 cup flour
1/2 teaspoon seasoned salt
1/4 teaspoon black pepper
1 teaspoon parsley flakes
1 teaspoon thyme
1 cup red wine
1/4 cup brandy

Coat fillets with softened butter. Mix flour, seasoned salt and pepper, dredge fillets. Grill or broil 3 minutes per side. Place breasts in dutch oven, add parsley, thyme and red wine. Cover and simmer for 30 minutes. Remove breasts and transfer to a warm serving platter. Over high heat boil liquid in dutch oven stirring constantly. Pour in brandy, remove from heat. Pour sauce over breasts.

Serve with your favorite vegetable and rice.

SAUTEED SNOW GOOSE

Simple but elegant.

breast fillet from 2 geese
1 package dry onion soup mix
2 tablespoons butter
1/4 teaspoon salt
1/4 teaspoon black pepper
1/2 cup water
3 tablespoons cooking sherry
1/2 cup cream

Rub fillets with softened butter. Place in casserole dish, sprinkle with salt and pepper and dry onion soup mix. Add 1/4 cup water, cover and bake at 325 for 35 minutes or until the meat is easily pierced with a fork.

Remove meat from casserole dish, slice thin and keep warm. Add sherry and cream to the juices in the casserole dish over medium heat. Stir briefly, pour over sliced meat.

OAHE CASSEROLE

use breast meat from pheasant, partridge, turkey
3 cups cooked, sliced meat
1 bunch fresh broccoli 1-1 1/2 lbs.
2 cans cream of chicken soup
1 cup mayonnaise
1 teaspoon lemon juice
1/2 cup shredded cheddar chees
1/2 cup soft bread croutons
1 tablespoon butter

Steam or boil until tender, about 20 minutes. Cool, remove from bone. Rinse broccoli, remove the large leaves and the heavy bottom stalk. Cut lengthwise from head through stalk. Arrange broccoli in a 9X13 pyrex baking pan. Place meat on top. Combine soup, mayonnaise, lemon juice, and pour over meat and broccoli. Sprinkle with cheese, combine croutons with butter and sprinkle over all. Bake uncovered 25-30 minutes at 350°.

CROCKED DUCK

2 ducks, quartered
1 medium onion, minced
1 stalk celery, minced
2 tablespoons butter
1/2 cup orange juice
1/2 teaspoon seasoned salt
1/4 teaspoon prepared mustard
1 tablespoon orange zest
1/4 cup heavy red wine or port

Melt butter over medium heat in medium sauce pan, add onion, celery and sauté gently. Add orange juice, seasoned salt, mustard, orange zest and wine. Place duck in crock pot, pour in sauce, cook on low heat for approx. 8 hours.

GOOSE FILLET WITH RICH SAUCE

breast fillets from 2 geese
4 tablespoons butter
1 carrot, minced
1 onion, minced
1 tablespoon parsley flakes
1 garlic clove, minced
3 tablespoons cooking oil
1/2 teaspoon worcestershire sauce
3 tablespoons catsup
1 cup water
2 beef bouillon cubes
1/3 cup orange juice
2/3 cup cream

Start by making the camp sauce: put carrot, onion, garlic, parsley flakes, oil, worcestershire sauce, catsup, water, bouillon in small skillet and cook over low heat for 30 minutes. Simultaneously spread butter on breast fillets and grill 4 inches over hot coals, 4 minutes per side. Remove fillets from grill and cut into thin slices, keep warm.

When camp sauce has cooked 30 minutes, add the orange juice and cream, continue cooking and stir for 2 minutes.

Serve camp sauce generously ladled over the sliced breast fillet.

LONG LAKE DUCK SOUP

breast fillets from 2 large ducks
3 cups water
1 teaspoon seasoned salt
1/2 teaspoon black pepper
1 carrot, chopped
1 celery stalk, chopped
1 green pepper, diced
3 cups milk
1 can chicken noodle soup
1 can cream of celery soup

Cut duck into bite size pieces. Combine meat, water, seasoned salt, pepper, carrot, celery and green pepper in large soup pot and slowly bring to a boil. Reduce heat, cover and simmer over low heat for 30 minutes. Add milk, canned soups. Stir and simmer for an additional 20 minutes.

CHARBROILED PINTAIL

2 ducks, skinned, split in half down the back
3 garlic cloves pressed, mashed
3 tablespoons butter
1/2 teaspoon paprika
1/2 teaspoon salt
1/4 teaspoon black pepper

Rub the ducks with garlic, place bone side down on well greased grill 4-5 inches above the coals for 15-18 minutes. Turn, baste with butter and broil an additional 8 minutes. Turn, baste with remaining butter and sprinkle with paprika, salt, pepper.

Serve with roast sweet corn and buttered squash.

FIELD AND STREAM GUMBO

This recipe offers an elegant alternative for preparing birds like sandhill cranes, hungarian partridge, or old long spurred pheasants.

1-2 lbs. wild fowl
2 quarts water
3 garlic cloves, pressed
1 large onion, chopped
1 green pepper, chopped
1 red pepper, chopped
4 stalks celery, chopped
1 cup fresh okra
2 large ripe tomatoes
1 tablespoon worcestershire sauce
1 teaspoon salt
1/2 teaspoon black pepper
1/3 cup uncooked barley or rice
1 lb medium shrimp peeled
1 lb fish fillets

Cook fowl in large kettle with water over moderate heat until it falls off the bone. Remove meat from bones, cut in small pieces, discard bones and return meat to kettle. Add garlic, onion, peppers, celery, okra, tomatoes, salt, worcestershire and pepper. Heat to boiling, reduce heat, cover and simmer 1 1/2 hours. Add barley and shrimp, simmer an additional 20 minutes. Cut fish into 1 inch pieces. Add to gumbo simmer an additional 6-8 minutes or until fish flakes easily. To thicken make a rue from 1 tablespoon oil and 2 tablespoons flour. Add liquid and stir into gumbo.

Serve over a bed of rice.

GOOSE LIVER PATE

(Appetizer)

livers and hearts from 3 geese
1 small onion, minced
1 hard boiled egg
2 teaspoons vermouth
2 tablespoons mayonnaise
salt, pepper to taste

In medium kettle boil the livers in water with the onion until tender. Remove from heat, cool. Place livers and hard boiled egg in blender and blend well using spatula to push mixture off sides into cutting blades. Remove from blender, place in a small bowl, add vermouth, mayonnaise, salt, pepper, stir until well blended. Chill in refrigerator before serving.

HORICON GOOSE FILLETS

6-8 breast fillets from geese or large ducks
1 cup flour
1 teaspoon
1/4 teaspoon freshly ground black pepper
5 tablespoons vegetable oil
1 large onion, minced
1/2 cup celery, minced
1/2 cup carrot, minced
1 cup dry white wine
1/4 cup + 2 tablespoons orange liqueur
1 1/2 cups stewed tomatoes
1 1/2 cups chicken broth
1/2 teaspoon basil
1/2 teaspoon rosemary
3 tablespoons grated orange peel (orange zest)
2 tablespoons cornstarch

Mix flour, salt, pepper, dredge meat and brown in oil over moderate heat in heavy dutch oven. Remove meat from pan, sauté onion, celery and carrot over moderate heat until onion is browned. Add the wine and 1/4 cup of orange liqueur and boil for 2 minutes, add chicken broth, tomatoes, herbs and orange zest. Add meat cover and bake at 350° for 1 1/2 to 2 hrs. or until tender. Transfer meat to a plate and keep warm.

In a small bowl, combine cornstarch and remaining 2 tablespoons of orange liqueur. Heat liquid in dutch oven to a boil, add the cornstarch mixture reduce heat, stir and simmer for 2-3 minutes or until thickened. Serve thickened sauce over meat.

Serve with fresh steamed vegetables.

PANCAKES · BISCUITS · VEGETABLES

The preceding recipes will stand alone in quality and taste. They will receive rave reviews and you, the cook, can enjoy the feeling of self-sufficing that accompanies the North American hunter and fisherman.

When planning your meal, consider your recipe needs and who you will be cooking for. Many times the best meal is one kept simple, that is, one where your main course isn't distracted by elaborate side dishes. When preparing stews or chili, simply add fresh baked bread. Rice, baked potato, fresh corn or squash will augment any recipe in this book. In addition, who can resist hot buttered noodles with a tender elk steak. Vegetables, including broccoli, brussels sprouts and peas, offer balanced nutrition, variety and color. Desserts made from wild berries are unquestionably terrific.

The recipes in this chapter are simple, nutritious, and tasty. They can be used to augment any meal or items such as pancakes can be the meal.

Use your imagination, recipes are guideposts. Keep it simple if you like, and enjoy.

HEARTLAND PANCAKES

1/2 cup buckwheat flour
1/2 cup unbleached all-purpose flour
1/4 cup whole wheat flour
1/4 cup ground almonds
2 tablespoons baking powder
1/2 teaspoon salt
2 eggs, separated
1 cup milk
2 tablespoons cooking oil

Mix together dry ingredients in medium sized bowl. In small bowl beat egg yolks, milk and cooking oil until well blended. Pour into the dry ingredients and stir until blended. Beat egg whites until stiff, fold into batter.

Lightly oil griddle over low - medium heat. Use about 3 tablespoons of batter per cake. Cook until several bubbles break the top, then turn, cook about a minute on the second side.

SOUR CREAM PANCAKES

1/2 cup sour cream
1/2 cup skim milk
2 eggs, separated
1 cup flour
1 teaspoon baking powder
1 tablespoon sugar
1/2 teaspoon salt
1/2 cup cooking oil

Mix sour cream, milk and eggs in a medium sized bowl. Add flour, baking powder, sugar, salt and mix. Add cooking oil and stir until smooth. Beat egg white until stiff and fold into batter. Lightly griddle over low - medium heat. Use 3 tablespoons batter per cake.

Cook until several bubbles break the surface of the cake, flip, cook about a minute on the second side.

JOHNNYCAKES

1 1/4 cup white cornmeal
1 tablespoon sugar
1 teaspoon salt
1 stick melted butter
1 1/2 cups boiling water

In medium bowl, mix cornmeal, sugar, salt, melted butter and pour in the boiling water. Beat with a spoon for 1 minute. Lightly oil griddle over low - medium heat, use 3 tablespoons batter per cake.

Cook until bottom is golden brown 6-8 minutes. Turn and cook second side.

POTATO PANCAKES

1/2 cup milk
3 eggs
4 1/2 cups grated potatoes
1 small grated onion
4 1/2 tablespoons flour
1 1/2 teaspoons salt
1/2 teaspoon baking powder

Mix all ingredients. Lightly oil griddle over medium heat. Pour on 2-3 tablespoons batter.

Cookl until golden brown, turning once.

CRANBERRY MUFFINS

1/2 stick butter
1/2 cup sugar
2 eggs
2 1/4 cups all-purpose flour
2 teaspoons baking powder
1/2 teaspoon salt
1 cup eggnog
1 cup cranberries, chopped
1/3 cup chopped pecans

Preheat oven to 350'. Cream butter and sugar, beat in eggs. Combine flour, baking powder and salt. Add dry ingredients and eggnog, mix well. Add cranberries and pecans.

Fill paper lined muffin cups 3/4 full. Bake 18 to 20 minutes.

BUTTERMILK BISCUITS

2 cups all-purpose flour
1 tablespoon baking powder
1 teaspoon salt
1/3 cup shortening
2/3 cup buttermilk

Preheat oven to 450˚. In medium bowl mix 1 1/2 cups flour, baking powder and salt. Cut in the shortening until the mixture resembles course meal. Stir in the buttermilk until thoroughly blended.

Turn dough out on a lightly floured surface and knead in the remaining 1/2 cup flour. Roll out the dough 1/2 inch thick. Cut 2 inch circles with cutter. Place 1 inch apart on a lightly greased pan and bake 10-12 minutes or until a light golden brown.

PRAIRIE BISCUITS

1 1/2 cups unbleached flour
2 1/4 teaspoons baking powder
3/4 teaspoon salt
1 cup cream
2 tablespoons butter

Preheat oven to 425˚. In medium bowl mix flour, baking powder and salt. Add cream and mix until blended.

With buttered hands, pinch off dough and shape 1 inch balls. Place on ungreased baking sheet 1 inch apart.

Bake for 10-12 minutes or until golden.

BAKING POWDER BISCUITS

2 cups unbleached flour
1 tablespoon baking powder
2 teaspoons sugar
1 teaspoon salt
1/3 cup vegetable shortening
2/3 cup milk
1 tablespoon melted butter

Preheat oven to 450°. In a medium bowl sift together the flour, baking poowder, sugar and salt. Cut in shortening until the mixture resembles coarse meal. Gradually stir in enough milk to make a soft, puffy pliable dough. Too much milk will make dough sticky.

Turn the dough out onto a lightly floured surface. Knead, lightly about 6 times. Roll out into a circle 1/2 inch thick. Brush surface with the melted butter. Fold the dough and again roll out into a circle 1/2 inch thick. Cut out using 2 inch cutter. Place on ungreased baking sheet. Bake for 10-12 minutes in the middle of the oven.

DAKOTA BREAD

This creation of the Dakota Wheat Commision is a grand accompaniment to any meal.

1 package active dry yeast
1/2 cup warm water
2 tablespoons sunflower oil
1 egg
1/2 cup cottage cheese
1/4 cup honey
1 teaspoon salt
2 1/2 cups bread flour
1/2 cup whole wheat flour
1/4 cup wheat germ
1/4 cup rye flour
1/4 cup rolled oats
cornmeal

Mix yeast in warm water and dissolve. In large bowl, mix sunflower oil, egg, cottage cheese, honey and salt. Add dissolved yeast and 2 cups flour, beat until flour is moistened. Gradually stir in whole wheat flour, wheat germ, rye flour and oats. Add enough bread flour to make dough soft and pliable.

Turn out on a floured surface, knead dough about 10 minutes or until dough is smoot. Place dough in greased bowl; cover loosely with oiled plastic wrap, let rise in warm place until dough doubles in size, about 30 minutes.

Punch down dough, shape into one round loaf, place in a greased glass pie pan sprinkled with cornmeal. Cover with oiled plastic wrap and let rise until double in size, about 1 hour. Brush with egg white and sprinkle with wheat germ and sunflower kernels. Bake at 350° for 35-40 minutes.

ALMOND POPPYSEED MUFFINS

2 cups flour
1/2 teaspoon salt
2 teaspoons baking powder
1 cup sugar
2 eggs
3 tablespoons poppy seeds
1/2 teaspoon baking soda
2 teaspoons almond extract
1/2 cup butter
1 cup plain yogurt

Preheat oven to 400°. Combine flour, salt, baking powder, baking soda and poppy seed in a medium sized bowl. Cream butter and sugar in a large bowl. Beat in eggs one at a time. Beat in yogurt and almond extract. Stir in the flour mixture just until moistened. Spoon into greased muffin tins.

Bake at 400° for 18-20 minutes.

Makes 12 muffins.

HUCKLEBERRY MUFFINS

2 1/2 cups flour
2 teaspoons baking powder
2 teaspoons baking soda
1 teaspoon salt
2 eggs
1 1/4 cup sugar
1 cup raw wheat bran
1 cup boiling water
2 cups buttermilk
3/4 cup vegetable oil
1 cup fresh huckleberries

In small bowl combine flour, baking powder, baking soda and salt.

In small bowl combine the wheat bran and water, mixing to assure that water is absorbed.

In large bowl, lightly beat eggs, sugar, oil and milk, stir in bran. Add the flour mixture and stir only until moistened. Lightly fold in the huckleberries. Chill the batter for several hours.

Preheat oven to 350°, spoon chilled batter into greased muffin pans. Bake at 350° for 25-30 minutes or until golden brown.

Makes 12 muffins.

LEMON POPPY SEED MUFFINS

2 cups flour
1 cup sugar
2 tablespoons brown sugar
1 tablespoon baking powder
1 teaspoon salt
3 tablespoons poppy seeds
1 egg
2/3 cup milk
1 teaspoon lemon zest
2 tablespoons lemon juice
1/2 cup oil

Preheat oven to 400°. Combine flour, sugar, baking powder, salt and poppy seeds in a medium sized bowl.

In seperate bowl lightly beat egg, milk, lemon zest, lemon juice and oil. Add liquid to the flour mixture, stirring just until moistened.

Spoon into greased muffin pan till about 3/4 full. Sprinkle 2 tablespoons of brown sugar lightly over the tops of the muffins.

Bake at 400° for 18-20 minutes.

Makes 12 muffins.

BRAN PANCAKES

1 egg
2 egg whites
1 cup milk
3 tablespoons vegetable oil
1 cup plain yogurt
1/4 cup honey
1 teaspoon vanilla
1 1/4 cups flour
1/2 cup raw oat bran
1/4 cup raw wheat bran
1 teaspoon baking powder
1 teaspoon baking soda
1/2 teaspoon salt

In large bowl, beat egg and egg whites until frothy, beat in milk, oil, yogurt, honey and vanilla until blended. Add flour, bran, baking powder, soda and salt, blend well.

Fry by pouring 3 tablespoons of batter on hot, lightly greased griddle.

BRAN MUFFINS

part I:
1 cup raw red bran
1 cup boiling water

Mix bran and boiling water, let stand.

part II
1/2 cup margarine
1 cup sugar
2 eggs
1 pint buttermilk
2 1/2 cups flour
2 1/2 teaspoons baking soda
1/4 teaspoon salt
2 cups all bran

Cream margarine with sugar, add eggs 1 at a time. Mix in buttermilk, flour, soda, salt and all bran. Stir well. Add bran water mixture from part I. Use as needed. Store in air tight container in refrigerator. Will keep up to 6 weeks.

Bake in greased muffin tins at 350° for 18-20 minutes.

JOAN'S BANANA OAT BRAN MUFFINS

3 medium bananas, mashed
2 egg whites
1/3 cup vegetable oil
3/4 teaspoon salt
1/2 cup sugar
1 cup flour
2 teaspoons baking powder
1/4 teaspoon baking soda
1/2 cup oat bran
1/4 cup toasted wheat germ
1/2 cup walnuts, chopped
1/2 cup dates, chopped

Heat oven to 350°. In medium bowl combine banana, egg whites and oil. Sift together salt, sugar, flour, baking powder and baking soda. Mix in all ingredients all at once and stir only until flour is moistened. The batter will be lumpy.

Fill muffin cups or greased muffin tins 3/4 full.

Bake 20-25 minutes or until golden brown.

IDAHO POTATO SALAD

6 medium potatoes, boiled, sliced
4 stalks celery, chopped
1 onion, chopped
1/2 green pepper, chopped
1/2 sweet red pepper, chopped
2 hardboiled eggs, sliced

dressing:
1 cup mayonnaise
2 tablespoons french style mustard
1/2 teaspoon salt
1/2 teaspoon black pepper
1/4 teaspoon paprika

In large bowl, lightly mix all vegetables. In small bowl mix the dressing ingredients. Fold the dressing into the vegetables, arrange sliced egg on top and sprinkle with paprika.

BUTTERED CRUMB NOODLES

A simple tasty addition to any game meal.

6 cups water
3 chicken bouillon cubes
8 oz. wide noodles
1 slice whole wheat bread, toasted, crumbed
4 tablespoons butter
salt and pepper

Bring water with bouillon cubes to a boil. Add noodles, cook 8-10 minutes or until tender. Sauté bread crumbs in 1 tablespoon butter until lightly browned.

Drain noodles, do not rinse, return noodles to original kettle, add remaining butter, salt and pepper to taste. Add bread crumbs.

LITE POTATO SALAD

6 medium potatoes, boiled, sliced
2 1/2 cups broccoli, steamed. chopped
1 onion, chopped
1/2 red pepper, chopped
2 hardboiled eggs, at least 1 yolk discarded

dressing:
1 cup nonfat plain yogurt
1 tablespoon koerner or dijon style mustard
1 teaspoon sugar
1 tablespoon lemon juice
1/2 teaspoon salt
1/2 teaspoon black pepper
1 teaspoon dill

In large bowl, lightly mix all vegetables. In small bowl mix the dressing ingredients. Fold the dressing into the vegetables, arrange sliced egg on top, sprinkle with paprika.

MUSHROOMS AND WILD RICE

1 pound fresh mushrooms, sliced
1/4 teaspoon lemon juice
4 tablespoons butter
1 cup sour cream
1/2 teaspoon salt
1/4 teaspoon pepper
2 cups cooked wild rice
2 cups cooked long grained rice

Melt butter over low heat in medium fry pan. Add mushrooms and lemon juice. Sauté gently until tender. Stir in sour cream, salt, pepper and rice.

BLACK DUCK WILD RICE SOUP

1 cup wild rice, rinsed
2 1/2 cups water
1 teaspoon basil
1 carrot, chopped
1 stalk celery, chopped
1 onion, minced
2 tablespoons butter
5 cups water
5-6 chicken bouillon cubes
dash of sage and thyme

In medium soup kettle combine 2 1/2 cups filtered (non-chlorinated) water, wild rice, basil, sage and thyme. Bring to boil, reduce heat and simmer 35 minutes.

In medium fry pan, melt butter over medium heat. Sauté carrots, celery, and onion until lightly browned. Add sauteed veggies to soup kettle. Add 5 additional cups of water and bouillon.

Simmer 20 minutes.

SQUASH CASSEROLE

4 cups squash, baked and cooled
3/4 cup sugar
3 eggs
1/2 cup cream
2 teaspoons vanilla
4 tablespoons margarine, melted

In large bowl mix all ingredients and beat until smooth. Put in 9X13 baking dish.

1/2 cup brown sugar
1/2 cup flour
1/2 stick margarine

Mix 1/2 cup brown sugar with 1/2 cup flour and sprinkle over top. Melt 1/2 stick margarine and drizzle over the top.

Bake at 325° for 1 hour.

STUFFED SQUASH

2 acorn squash
1 medium onion, minced
1 tablespoon cooking oil
1 stalk celery, minced
3/4 lb. ground turkey
1 tablespoon flour
3 tablespoons soy sauce

Cut squash in half lengthwise, remove seeds. Cover with plastic wrap, microwave on high for 4 minutes or until tender.

Heat cooking oil over medium heat in heavy fry pan. Sauté onion and celery until lightly brown. Add turkey, cook and stir 3-5 minutes. Sprinkle flour, stir to blend. Stir in soy sauce. Remove from heat, fill cavity in each squash half.

Cover and return to microwave for 1 minute on high setting.

FRIED POTATOES

A campsite favorite.

6 medium potatoes peeled, sliced
4 tablespoons vegetable oil
1 large onion, chopped
1/2 teaspoon salt
1/4 teaspoon black pepper

Fry sliced potatoes in heavy frypan over medium heat. Turn as potatoes on bottom become golden brown. When potatoes are done, add onion and fry an additional 5 minutes turning frequently.

HOMESTEAD RICE

4 tablespoons margarine
1 medium onion, minced
1/2 teaspoon salt
1/4 teaspoon black pepper
1/4 cup worcestershire sauce
1 garlic clove, minced
2 cups hot water
1 cup long grained rice

Melt margarine in a 2 quart kettle over medium heat. Sauté onion gently until lightly brown. Add salt, pepper, worcestershire sauce and minced garlic.

Add hot water, bring to boil over high heat. Stir in rice, return to boil.

Cover and simmer 15-20 minutes until all water is absorbed.

VEGETABLE CASSEROLE

4 carrots, chopped
1 bunch broccoli
3 tablespoons butter
1/2 head cauliflower
3 tablespoons flour
1 1/2 cups milk
3/4 cup cubed cheese
1 cup croutons

Steam vegetables until tender. Make cream sauce by melting butter in medium sauce pan over medium heat. Stir in flour, add milk and cheese, reduce heat. Cook and stir until creamy. Place vegetables in casserole dish, pour over cream sauce.

Sprinkle with croutons. Bake at 300° for 15-20 minutes.

BAKED CORN

1 can creamed corn
1/2 cup saltine crumbs
2 eggs, beaten
1 1/2 cups milk
salt and pepper

Mix all ingredients in casserole dish. Bake at 350° for 15-20 minutes or until top is lightly browned.

DUTCH OVEN BEANS

1 lb. large white (navy) beans
6 slices bacon
3/4 cup molasses
1/2 cup catsup
2 onions, chopped
1 teaspoon koerner style mustard
1 tablespoon salt
1/2 teaspoon black pepper
1/2 cup water

Wash and soak beans for 2-4 hours, drain beans and place in dutch oven. Cut bacon and onion and mix with beans. Mix molasses, catsup and all seasonings with the water and pour over beans.

If camping, bury in hot coals for 6 hours. If using a conventional oven bake at 350° for approx. 4-6 hours or until tender.

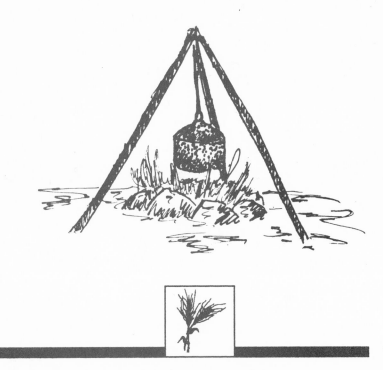

WILD BERRIES

Wild berries grow practically everywhere you find untilled soil. They provide sustenance for wildlife and properly prepared can provide the basis for sensational eating.

Jams and jellies made from fresh wild berries will be delicious if you gather the fruit when ripe and process as soon as possible. Properly canned, sealed and stored, your prize will keep till the next growing season.

However, it is important to know the berries you are picking are edible and safe. A prime example is the chokecherry where the pulp of the berry is edible but the stone or pit can be poisonous. A little research and experimentation will suffice and treat you and your family to a gratifying wild experience.

CHOKECHERRY JELLY

Pick fruit from trees when the berries are plump and ripe, the more ripe the berries the better your jelly. Over ripe or dented berries should be left for the birds. A 5 quart pail of berries will yield a quart of good juice.

3 cups juice
6 1/2 cups sugar
2 packages "certo" liquid pectin

making juice:

Wash fruit well and drain, place in an enamel kettle and cook over low heat. Add only about a cup of water and crush fruit to speed the process. Cook until the fruit is soft and begins to lose its color. Strain juice through a pre-moistened jelly bag into a clean container. Let juice drip as long as feasable.

making jelly:

Measure the strained juice into a large enamel kettle. Heat and simmer uncovered for 5 minutes. Skim off any froth. Add sugar and stir with a wooden spoon until it is dissolved. Bring to a quick boil stirring constantly. Add pectin and boil hard for one minute.

Remove from heat, skim froth. Fill sterilized jars. Seal jars, store in a cool, dark, dry place.

BULL BERRY JELLY

The common practice for gathering this fruit is to wait until after the first frost then spread a sheet under the fruit laden bush and shake it. The good fruit can be separated from the leaves, twigs and over-ripe fruit by running water in a large pail filled with berries. The junk will float to the top leaving the good berries on the bottom of the pail.

6 cups juice
7 1/2 cups sugar
1 box sure-jell
1/2 teaspoon butter

making juice:
Follow the process described for making chokecherry juice.

making jelly:
Measure the sugar into a separate bowl. Measure the strained juice into a large enamel kettle. Add one box sure-jell pectin and 1/2 teaspoon butter. Bring mixture to a full rolling boil over high heat, stirring constantly. Quickly add sugar, bring to a full rolling boil for 1 minute, stir continuously.

Remove from heat, skim off froth, fill sterilized jars. Seal jars, store in a cool, dark, dry place.

WILD ROSE-HIP JAM

Hips from the roses that grow wild are readily transformed into a delicious jam. For the best results wait until after the first frost before you pick the little bulb like hips from the rose.

1 lb. rose hips
1 cup water
1 lb. sugar

making jam:
Wash the hips well and drain. Place in large enamel kettle. Add 1 cup water, crush the hips and simmer uncovered until hips become soft. Remove from heat, rub through a fine sieve.

Weigh the pulp, add one pound of sugar for each pound of pulp. Over medium heat bring the mixture to a boil and continue to stir. Reduce heat and continue to cook uncovered until the mixture thickens (may take up to 1/2 hour).

Remove from heat, skim froth.

Fill sterilized jars and store in cool, dark, dry place.

RASPBERRY CREAM PIE

1 9 inch pie crust, baked
1 3 oz. package vanilla pudding mix
1 1/2 cups milk
1/4 teaspoon almond extract
1 cup cool whip
3 cups raspberries
1 tablespoon sugar
1 tablespoon cornstarch
1 teaspoon lemon zest
1 tablespoon lemon juice
1/2 cup water

Prepare pudding using only 1 1/2 cups milk, stir in almond extract, cover and refrigerate 1 hour.

Fold cool whip into pudding. Spoon into pie crust, refrigerate.

Sort berries, save 2 cups of the best. Use 1 cup of berries, place in medium sauce pan with sugar, cornstarch, lemon zest, lemon juice and water, stir over medium heat until mixture thickens, remove from heat, cool. Fold in remaining 2 cups of berries, spoon over pudding in pie shell, refrigerate 4-6 hours.

HUCKLEBERRY PIE

40 vanilla wafers
1/3 cup melted butter
1/2 teaspoon unflavored gelatin
1/2 cup butter
1 1/2 cups powdered sugar
2 beaten eggs
1 pint cool whip
2 cups huckleberries

Crush the wafers into fine crumbs, combine with 1/3 cup melted butter and gelatin. Mix thoroughly and press into 9 in. pie plate. Chill 1 hour.

Cream 1/2 cup butter, add powdered sugar and 2 beaten eggs. Beat on high speed until fluffy, pour into crust and smooth top.

Blend the huckleberries with the cool whip and spoon over the top of the pie.

Sprinkle additional wafer crumbs on top, chill 4-6 hours.

ELDERBERRY JELLY

4 quarts fresh elderberries
6 cups water
6 cups sugar
1 pouch liquid pectin

Clean the berries, remove all stems and leaves, place in enamel kettle, add water and bring to a boil over high heat. Reduce heat to medium and cook uncovered for 45 minutes stirring occasionally.

Strain fruit through jelly bag to extract juice.

Rinse out kettle.

Measure juice and return to kettle for each cup of juice, add 1 1/2 cups sugar. Stir to dissolve sugar, bring to heavy rolling boil, boil hard for 1 minute, add pectin, boil and additional minute. Remove from heat, skim off froth.

Pour jelly into sterilized jars, cover and seal. Place sealed jars of hot jam on a rack in a canner kettle with boiling water. Water should cover the jars. Boil for 14 minutes. Remove from heat, let stand to cool.

BLACKBERRY JAM

2 quarts fresh blackberries
7 cups sugar
1 pouch certo liquid pectin
1/2 teaspoon butter

Thoroughly crush berries, put half of berries through a sieve to remove some of the seeds. Measure 4 cups of fruit into an enamel kettle. Add sugar and butter and bring to a full rolling boil, stirring constantly, continue to boil for 1 minute. Remove from heat, stir in pectin, skim foam and fill sterilized jars. Cover and seal.

Place sealed jars of hot jam on a rack in a canner kettle with boiling water. Water should cover the jars. Boil for 5 minutes. Remove from heat, let jam stand to cool, store in a cool, dark, dry place.

PRAIRIE BERRY JELLY

This recipe blends the chokecherry with the bullberry or buffalo berry and makes an exquisite jelly.

5 cups bull or buffalo berry juice
1 cup chokecherry juice
7 1/2 cups sugar
1 box sure-jell pectin
1/2 teaspoon butter

making jelly:

Measure the sugar into a separate bowl. Measure the strained juice into a large enamel kettle. Add one box pectin and 1/2 teaspoon butter. Bring mixture to a full rolling boil over high heat, stirring constantly. Add sugar, stir to dissolve and bring to full rolling boil and continue to stir and cook for one minute.

Remove from heat, skim off froth, fill sterilized jars, seal jars, store in cool, dark place.

WILD STRAWBERRY PIE

9 inch pie crust, baked
1 qt. strawberries, washed, picked, stems removed
1 cup sugar
2 tablespoons butter
3 tablespoons corn starch
1 teaspoon lemon juice
3 oz. cream cheese

Spread cream cheese over the crust, arrange 1/2 of the berries over the cream cheese.

In medium sauce pan combine remaining berries, sugar, cornstarch and lemon juice. Mash the berries, and stirring constantly bring to a boil, lower heat, stir and cook for an additional 3 minutes. Remove from heat, stir in butter, cool for 20 minutes, spread over pie.

Chill and serve with whipped cream.

ORDER INFORMATION

You may order additional copies of this book for
$12.95 each plus $2.55 shipping by sending
your name, address and payment to:

Adventure Publications
P.O. Box 269
Cambridge, MN 55008
or
You can use your MasterCard or VISA by
calling 1-800-678-7006

Copies of the new
"A Sportsman's Journal"

may be obtained for $15.95 plus $3.95 shipping
by phone or mail from Adventure Publications.